STANDING STRONG

How to Storm-Proof Your Life
with God's Timeless Truths

CHARLES F. STANLEY

HOWARD BOOKS
AN IMPRINT OF SIMON & SCHUSTER, INC.

New York   London   Toronto   Sydney   New Delhi

Howard Books
An Imprint of Simon & Schuster, Inc.
1230 Avenue of the Americas
New York, NY 10020

First Howard Books hardcover edition October 2017

HOWARD and colophon are trademarks of Simon & Schuster, Inc.

For information about special discounts for bulk purchases, please
contact Simon & Schuster Special Sales at
1-866-506-1949 or business@simonandschuster.com.

The Simon & Schuster Speakers Bureau can bring authors to your live event.
For more information or to book an event, contact the Simon & Schuster Speakers
Bureau at 1-866-248-3049 or visit our website at www.simonspeakers.com.

Interior design by Jason Snyder

Manufactured in the United States of America

10 9 8 7 6 5 4 3 2 1

Library of Congress Control Number: 2017036941

ISBN 978-1-5011-7739-2
ISBN 978-1-5011-7741-5 (ebook)

CONTENTS

STANDING
STRONG

1

TWO WAYS TO BUILD

Strength or Weakness—It's Your Choice

A strong life.
A life that endures.
A life that makes an eternal impact.

I think all of us would agree that's the kind of existence we wish to have—one that has a lasting influence on this world and beyond. We want to know that the days we live are actually making a difference and that there is a reason for what we do and for the difficulties we experience. We want to be sure that what we are standing for is worthwhile.

But we also understand that to do so, we must break free from the factors that make us weak—those issues that hold us back and undermine us.

Because the truth of the matter is, it usually isn't when we're feeling tough and confident that we go looking for books on *standing strong*. It's not when we're secure and assured that we need encouragement. Rather, it's when the future is unsure. We become aware that we might not be as successful as we thought, and we long to know how to make it through—and how to do so well. It's

1

when the burdens get heavy, the challenges we face seem impossible, or the obstacles that stare at us from the horizon appear overwhelming. That's when we realize that we are in danger of being less than we'd hoped to be or, worse, failing altogether. That's when we reach out for wisdom about how to stand.

Whether we are eight years old, forty-eight, or eighty-eight, in the core of our hearts, we don't want failure to characterize the end of our stories. We don't want to be known for our worst mistakes and defeats, but for our greatest victories and triumphs.

When we realize that we are in danger of being less than we'd hoped to be or, worse, failing altogether— that's when we reach out for wisdom about how to stand.

So what goes into the construction of a strong life? It's not just having a healthy body—that's useful, but there is much more to it than that. Likewise, it is more than having a good job, plenty of money, or prestigious social standing in your community. How can you experience a strong, fruitful life? What does it take?

A LESSON FROM ARCHITECTURE: A STABLE FOUNDATION

To understand this, we can take a lesson from architecture, since we know what it takes to raise a strong building. In fact, it is a useful exercise to look at the edifices around us and throughout the world and consider what causes some structures to endure throughout the centuries of bad weather and harsh elements and others to topple within years of their construction. Naturally, we cannot go into a detailed examination of this topic. But what are the basic reasons some buildings can withstand the poundings of the harshest elements and others fail at the onset of bad weather?

The most important factor, of course, is a stable foundation.

We sometimes see tragically sad reports in the news. A two-story island resort in Thailand collapses without warning. A six-story building in Nairobi falls unexpectedly, killing twelve. A tenement building in New Delhi crashes to the ground, taking the lives of sixty-seven. Why? In such cases, heavy rains compromised already weak foundations and caused them to fall.

We can see this in Israel and the Middle East, which experience seasons of severe storms and torrential rainfall. During such times, the landscape can change dramatically. The sunbaked ground, which seems so solid during the lengthy dry seasons, easily gives way when the raging waters pound against it. Gullies are formed as the force of the floods makes a path through whatever yields to it. Anything built on those shifting sands ultimately falls.

Obviously, this is a problem for anyone who wishes to build any kind of permanent structure. If they want to ensure that their buildings will last, they must take more time, invest the additional resources, and make the extra effort to drill down past the layers of compacted sediment and anchor the structure to the immovable rock.

The same is true for our lives. Jesus explained it like this:

"Everyone who hears these words of Mine and acts on them, may be compared to a wise man who built his house on the rock. And the rain fell, and the floods came, and the winds blew and slammed against that house; and yet it did not fall, for it had been founded on the rock. Everyone who hears these words of Mine and does not act on them, will be like a foolish man who built his house on the sand. The rain fell, and the floods came, and the winds blew and slammed against that house; and it fell—and great was its fall." (Matt. 7:24–28)

No one is exactly sure where Jesus taught the Sermon on the Mount, but wherever that location was, we know it was near the Sea of Galilee and close to Capernaum, and Christ's listeners would have witnessed a visual representation of this truth. The surrounding landscape appeared safe, but in fact builders were required to dig down to the bedrock in order for the structures to remain secure. Perhaps they had even seen the remains of buildings that had been poorly founded on the sand and had slid and tumbled when the storms rolled in.

Yet we must understand that even though Jesus is talking about an outward reality of a building's foundation, He is also describing an internal truth—the importance of what we base our lives on and who we are on the inside.

Understand, I am not talking merely about a backbone issue. It's not just about sticking to your ideals when the bad times come. We have all seen people who outwardly cling to their ideologies and values while privately turning to destructive coping mechanisms, hurting their relationships, or crumbling emotionally. Rather, the choices you make about what you believe go to the heart of who you are as a person. You can stand strong on the outside because, on the inside, your life is established on unshakable, unfailing truth. It matters what you believe and why you believe it.

When suffering and disappointments come our way, if our lives are built on the right foundation, we can stand no matter what happens. If they're not, we won't. Oh, we may look sturdy while the sun is shining and everything is going our way, but when the winds and rains start pounding down, who we really are is evident. And sometimes, that's not a very good picture.

Some people, when renovating a house, upgrade only the cosmetic aspects—new hedges, nicer tiling, perhaps some enhanced lighting. They may also try to hide the defects with paint or cleverly positioned furniture and artwork.

So it is when we "renovate" our lives—we may try to get in shape, improve our health, dress nicer, embellish our résumé, and even become more outwardly religious. We try to impress others with our external qualities. We may also try to mask or diminish our pain, weaknesses, and fears with addictive substances or immoral behavior—hoping that, somehow, they'll make us more courageous. But they don't. They undermine our confidence even further.

All the while, we know that we actually need to replace the foundation and fix those things deep within us that are broken. But that is much more costly, and we wonder if anyone would even notice if we made the sacrifices to improve.

We actually need to replace the foundation and fix those things deep within us that are broken.

Sadly, no matter how attractive a house is, if the foundation isn't solid, it will fall. This is one of the most important principles any of us will ever learn: Our life must be built on the right foundation.

Jesus says that if we want to withstand the inevitable storms, our lives must be based on something that cannot be moved—something that nothing in eternity can overturn. And friend, the only thing that will last forever is an intimate relationship with God. We may be drawn to things that promise to endure a long time, but nothing in this world will outlast the Lord Almighty.

Psalm 90:2 reminds us that God existed before the dawn of time and will continue to remain when time itself is no more: "Before the mountains were born or You gave birth to the earth and the world, even from everlasting to everlasting, You are God."

And, of course, from a verse many of us can quote, we know that He offers us an unshakable relationship with Himself: "God so loved the world, that He gave His only begotten Son, that whoever believes in Him shall not perish, but have eternal life" (John 3:16).

That whoever believes in Him shall not perish. Shall not topple or crash when the storms of life assail.

That whoever believes in Him shall . . . have eternal life. Shall have a life that endures—that is counted in eternity.

So this is the very first step to having a strong life and an unshakable foundation—having a relationship with God, which can come only through the death of Jesus on the cross. Friend, if you have never accepted Jesus as your Savior and Lord—trusting in Him *alone* for your salvation—then you're not building on the right foundation.

Why? Because if you don't know Jesus, you are building on your own nature, which is damaged and unreliable. No one has to tell you what your sins, failings, and mistakes are; they come immediately to mind, no matter how hard you try to forget them. Likewise, you must understand that your own nature is limited and inadequate—not only can you not see the future or control anything outside of your immediate scope of influence, but you will die one day. Any foundation you can come up with by yourself can only be temporary and insufficient.

The first step to having a strong life and an unshakable foundation is having a relationship with God, which can come only through the death of Jesus on the cross.

But Jesus, through His death on the cross, does these two things:

First, Jesus eliminates that old, defective foundation and pays the penalty for everything you have ever done wrong. Your sins separate you from God—from the only One who is holy, eternal, and unlimited, and who can make your life strong. You need Christ to haul all of that old, collapsing, decaying foundation away.

Second, Jesus makes you spiritually and eternally alive. He gives you a new nature and, therefore, a new foundation on which to establish your life.

Understanding this is at the heart of accepting what Jesus has done for you. Some people believe that following God is simply about observing the guidelines He has given in His Word. That is certainly part of it. But unless you are spiritually alive through the salvation Jesus offers you, you don't really have a relationship with God. You are merely submitting to rules.

KICKING AGAINST THE GOADS

Perhaps one of the best examples of the necessity of knowing God through a new foundation is the apostle Paul. Most people would recognize the apostle Paul as a man who stood strong—and I would heartily agree with them. After all, apart from Jesus, few have had such an incredible influence on the church as he has. Paul went on three fruitful missionary journeys; founded many churches, which, in turn, planted many more; and wrote almost half of the New Testament. Certainly, we can say that the life of the apostle Paul continues to have a powerful impact to this day.

But we also need to recognize that his story could have ended very differently.

At one time, Paul was called Saul, and he had all the prestige this world had to offer. He was a respected member of one of the most powerful religious ruling classes, the Pharisees. He was trained under Gamaliel, one of the greatest rabbis of the first century. Saul was known and admired among his peers as a faithful and talented man who was full of zeal for his nation.

In fact, Saul was so passionate about his beliefs that he was willing to kill for them. As a committed Jew, he observed the laws of God to the letter. He also persecuted the newfound Christian church and was even present for the execution of the first Christian martyr, Stephen (Acts 7:59–8:1). Those in his community may have thought Saul had it all—he was a religious giant and a force to be reckoned with. And the reality is that we might have thought so as well. We might have looked at Saul and seen a wealthy, educated man with a lot of power and an untouchable pedigree.

But we would have been looking at the wrong things. The truth of the matter was that Saul was on track for a life full of futility, weakness, murder, and regret. Yes, Saul was committed *to* God, but he did not truly have a relationship *with* Him.

Thankfully, that was all before Saul met Jesus and became Paul.

Perhaps you recall the story. "As he was traveling, it happened that he was approaching Damascus, and suddenly a light from heaven flashed around him; and he fell to the ground and heard a voice saying to him, 'Saul, Saul, why are you persecuting Me?' And [Saul] said, 'Who are You, Lord?' And He said, 'I am Jesus whom you are persecuting'" (Acts 9:3–5).

The man who was willing to do anything for God finally met Him face-to-face on that road to Damascus. And that meeting completely transformed his life.

Later, when Paul retells the story, he includes an interesting detail. He says, "I heard a voice saying to me in the Hebrew dialect, 'Saul, Saul, why are you persecuting Me? It is hard for you to kick against the goads'" (Acts 26:14).

It is hard for you to kick against the goads.

Unless you raise cattle, that phrase probably does not have much meaning. Farmers use a goad to direct oxen or other beasts of burden as they plow fields. Usually it is a stick with a pointed piece of metal on the end that the farmer can use as a prod. A rebellious ox might fight back, kicking against the goad, which actually drives the sharp iron tip deeper into the animal's flesh, injuring it. The more the ox fights, the more it wounds and weakens itself.

The picture is striking. Saul thought he was living a strong life *for* God because of his legalistic adherence to the Law, which is the tool—or goad—that the Lord uses to direct us in how to walk with Him. But Paul was really fighting *against* the goad—against Scripture—because Scripture's true purpose has always been to lead humanity to the salvation Jesus offers (Rom. 7:7–25).

So Paul's erroneous beliefs (and the acceptance of his fellow Pharisees) were actually weakening him, undermining his life and his relationship with the Lord. He missed the very Messiah God's Word was pointing to (John 5:39)! We will talk about this in detail in the next chapter.

But I wonder how many people reading this book are doing the same? Following God but not really knowing Him. Wanting to build an admirable and joyous life but ending up with destruction and despair. Thinking they are living for the Lord but unwittingly allowing their faulty beliefs to undermine their lives and relationship with Him. Like Paul, *kicking against the goads*.

Friend, is this you? Are you a moral person who lives a good life—loving others and doing what you think is right but finding a lack of strength, joy, or meaning in your daily existence? Do you know *of* God but not know *Him* personally? Do you find a lack of stability, security, or purpose in your life? Are you missing His presence, provision, and peace?

Like Paul, you can change course. You need to start by looking closely at yourself: Are you just observing Judeo-Christian rules without actually having a personal relationship with God Himself? This comes through accepting Jesus Christ, acknowledging Him as your Lord and Savior. As Paul says in 1 Corinthians 3:11, "No man can lay a foundation other than the one which is laid, which is Jesus Christ."

Do you know of God but not know Him personally? Are you missing His presence, provision, and peace?

So how do you do this? How do you make a relationship with Christ your foundation? It is as simple as talking to Him. You can tell Him in your own words or use this simple prayer:

Lord Jesus, I want a relationship with God—I want to build my life on the eternal foundation that You offer. Lord Jesus, please forgive my sins and remove the old foundation of my sinful nature. Save me from eternal separation from God. By faith, I accept Your work and death on the cross as sufficient payment for all my sins, mistakes, and failings. Thank You for making me spiritually alive—providing the way for me to know You and to have a relationship with my heavenly Father. Through faith in You, I have eternal life and an everlasting foundation for my life. Thank You for saving me! Jesus, I acknowledge You as the Lord of my life. Identify my false beliefs so I will stop kicking against the goads and wounding myself. Help me to live a strong life that is worthy of You and the new nature You have given me. Please give me the strength, wisdom, and determination to walk in the center of Your will. In Jesus' name, amen.

BUILDING OR UNDERMINING

If you've just received Jesus as your Lord and Savior, you've made the very best decision you will ever make. There is absolutely nothing more important than having a personal relationship with God. This is the firm foundation that the rest of your life will be built on. You simply cannot have a strong life without Him. Thankfully, now you are on the path to having the resilient and meaningful life you long for.

Of course, you may be thinking, *I accepted Jesus a long time ago. I've built my life on God, but I still feel weak.* Perhaps you have known Christ since you were a small child or grew up in a Christian home and truly believe everything you do has a godly basis.

But consider: *Does what you believe really line up with the Word of God?* After all, Saul, too, was wholeheartedly convinced he was doing right. That is, until he had a true encounter with Jesus.

Friend, we need to be conscious of the fact that, sometimes, we may be kicking against the goads of Scripture, by holding to beliefs that are actually weakening us. We need to measure everything we hold dear against the truth of Scripture and not just take what we've been taught at face value. Why? Because at times we hold beliefs that are actually contrary to God's Word—whether because we were taught them by someone we respect or because our experiences have shaped our understanding. By holding to wrong beliefs, we become weaker.

Let's go back to what Jesus said in the Sermon on the Mount: "Everyone who hears these words of Mine and acts on them, may be compared to a wise man who built his house on the rock" (Matt. 7:24). The only basis for a rock-solid foundation is God's Word. Not what your parents taught you. Not what your pastor said. Not even what you read in Christian books. *Everything* must be tested against God's Word (Acts 17:11).

Because the truth of the matter is that we are living in an age when taking Scripture seriously is becoming rarer and rarer. Some Christian leaders distance themselves from the Bible and turn to empty ideas and theories, sanctioning behavior that the Word of God condemns. Trust me, in the eight decades I have been alive, I have seen more church-building fads and philosophies come and go than I can count. Only one source has stood the test of time, and that is the Word of God.

So if your life is built on the temporary—read, *contemporary*—sand of passing opinions or other people's theology rather than a personal relationship with Jesus Christ, you may find yourself crumbling under the pressures of life.

The only basis for a rock-solid foundation is God's Word.

But if you build your life on the rock of truth—the Word of God, which has withstood the hurricane winds and torrential rains of time—not only will you stand in this life and even become better with the tempests, but your existence will make a difference in eternity.

This is why, in this book, we will take a long look into our *convictions*—the beliefs that influence our lives and shape our decisions. Our convictions define who we are and what we become—whether we become strong or weak, whether we build on or undermine the foundation of Christ. We live out our convictions every day in innumerable ways. So in Part 1 of this book, we will examine what our lives are *built on*: our most foundational views about the Trinity—God the Father, Son, and Holy Spirit—as well as what we really believe about Scripture and prayer.

A SECOND LESSON FROM ARCHITECTURE: THE RIGHT BUILDING DESIGN AND MATERIALS

Naturally, anyone who has ever built any kind of structure knows that it's not just what you build *on* that counts, but also *how* you build and what you build *with*. For example, in the last few decades there have been many advancements in hurricane- and earthquake-proofing houses. The right building materials used with the appropriate techniques can make a tremendous difference in the strength of a structure. We've all heard the stories and seen the photos on the news about the one house in a neighborhood that stands because of wise construction, while the rest are destroyed by storm-driven winds.

This leads us to our second factor in establishing a strong life, which is building it with the right methods and materials.

Paul echoes this idea:

If any man builds on the foundation with gold, silver, precious stones, wood, hay, straw, each man's work will become evident; for the day will show it because it is to be revealed with fire, and the fire itself will test the quality of each man's work. If any man's work which he has built on it remains, he will receive a reward. If any man's work is burned up, he will suffer loss; but he himself will be saved, yet so as through fire. (1 Cor. 3:12–15)

Of course, Paul is speaking about how we choose to construct our lives once the foundation of salvation through Christ is set.

We can either use materials based on our own ego, needs, and desires (wood, hay, and straw), which will eventually perish, or we can build our lives out of what will please God and will endure eternally (gold, silver, and precious stones).

Thankfully, once we accept Christ as our foundation, the right building materials and appropriate techniques will fall into place—if we will truly entrust our entire lives to Him.

Returning to Matthew 7:24, notice again what Jesus says: "Everyone who hears these words of Mine and acts on them, may be compared to a wise man who built his house on the rock." So, once you *hear* Him, you must *act on* what He's said if you are to be truly wise. James 1:22 echoes His message: "Prove yourselves doers of the word, and not merely hearers who delude themselves."

Once we accept Christ as our foundation, the right building materials and appropriate techniques will fall into place—if we will truly entrust our entire lives to Him.

You must allow what He says to change how you function. You must allow God's Word to transform you, because in it are the building design and materials that will last into eternity—when time is no more.

After all, why would you go through the trouble of laying a magnificent foundation and then build it with methods and materials that are sure to fail? That would make no sense.

And yet, that is what many Christians do. They lay their foundation on Christ but still miss some of the greatest joys a believer can experience by compartmentalizing their lives—deciding what behaviors and beliefs belong to God and which ones don't. They then pick and choose what they will or will not obey. This technique never *strengthens* a life, it only *tears* it down.

DESIRED OR LITTLE?

Again, we can look to Saul to illustrate this point. The name Saul means "desired or asked for." And certainly, that's what he was. People wanted to know him and sought his counsel and favor. In Philippians 3, Paul describes his résumé as a Pharisee—one that would impress anyone in that day:

> If others have reason for confidence in their own efforts, I
> have even more! I was circumcised when I was eight days
> old. I am a pure-blooded citizen of Israel and a member of
> the tribe of Benjamin—a real Hebrew if there ever was one!
> I was a member of the Pharisees, who demand the strictest
> obedience to the Jewish law. I was so zealous that I harshly
> persecuted the church. And as for righteousness, I obeyed
> the law without fault. (vv. 4–6 NLT)

These credentials may not mean too much to people today, but in Paul's time they meant he was the cream of the crop—an important man who had the respect of those who knew him. He had everything this world says is vital to being significant. We can understand how invigorating this was for him. After all, who doesn't want to be known for how bright, wealthy, important, powerful, spiritual, or attractive he or she is?

And yet, do you know what Paul said about all that?

I once thought these things were valuable, but now I consider them worthless because of what Christ has done. Yes, everything else is worthless when compared with the infinite value of knowing Christ Jesus my Lord. For his sake *I have discarded everything else*, counting it all as garbage, so that I could gain Christ. (vv. 7–8 NLT; emphasis added)

Do not miss this. Paul had to rethink *everything* he thought was true about what gave his life strength and value, not just some of what he believed. Notice that he said, "*I have discarded everything else*, counting it all as garbage."

And when he did, he went from *desired* Saul—the man who was sought after for his own worth—to Paul, which means "small or little." He became a man who became known for belonging to Jesus.

In fact, the name *Paul* is a derivative of the word *paúō*, which means "to cease or desist." What an incredible illustration of how his focus changed. He went from building his life on his own strengths, wisdom, and virtues to ceasing to be of importance at all—to considering himself nothing so Christ could have preeminence in his life. He as much said this when he wrote, "I do not consider my life of any account as dear to myself, so that I may finish my course and the ministry which I received from the Lord Jesus" (Acts 20:24). All of his dreams, all of his understanding, anything he could point to as giving him worth—every bit of it became nothing because Jesus became everything.

John the Baptist echoed this understanding when he said, "He must increase, but I must decrease" (John 3:30).

And that, friend, gave their lives incredible, everlasting strength.

Why? Paul himself wrote, "Because the foolishness of God is wiser than men, and the weakness of God is stronger than men" (1 Cor. 1:25). In other words, the life the Lord builds in us is always tougher and longer lasting than anything any person can ever achieve—no matter how mighty, important, affluent, influential, or intelligent he or she may be.

You and I must make this exchange as well. If we want to become strong, we have to change the focus from ourselves to the Lord; we must exchange our understanding for God's. And we must accept what He says *fully*—not holding back any area of our lives from His scrutiny and wisdom.

The life the Lord builds in us is always tougher and longer lasting than anything any person can ever achieve.

So, in Part 2 of this book, we will look at your convictions concerning obedience, the church, adversity, and the end of this life. Each one of these areas will show whether you are seeking to be *desired* for your own value or have made yourself *small* so God can be glorified. And how you look at each of these areas will make a tremendous difference in how sturdy your life is and whether it will bear fruit that lasts.

THE CHALLENGE TO STAND STRONG

Now, I understand that all of this will appear radical and counter-intuitive to some. And it is. What Jesus taught always requires faith that God truly exists and that He means what He says (Heb. 11:6). Likewise, not everyone will be able to accept how essential it is to trust Christ fully and stand on God's Word (John 6:44–69). Fears of criticism, rejection, failure, or loss will always stop some people from going forward on the path that God has for their lives. They won't want to become small so that the surpassing greatness of Christ can shine through them (2 Cor. 4:7). They won't be willing to give up their opinions and dreams so that God can achieve exceedingly greater goals through them. And they will continue in their weakness.

But if we want to have strong lives, we *have* to do something different from what we're already doing. As we said in the beginning, it's not just having a healthy body, a profitable profession, wealth, or significant social standing in your community. It takes something more, something beyond us that nothing can overturn.

Perhaps you've experienced all these earthly trappings that are supposed to give you strength and find them sadly lacking. Or maybe you're facing a terrible trial and are desperate for advice on how to make it through. Understanding how to stand strong is never more important than when the storms of life rage against us.

It could even be that you want to be prepared for the great plans God has for you. You've seen the difficulties and challenges great leaders face and want to make sure you have what it takes to endure and become all you were created to be. You desire to walk with a sense of purpose. You long to understand what speeds you along God's path and what hinders you from moving forward. You yearn to have the courage and confidence to endure when obstacles and people arise to challenge you.

Even as the best meteorologists cannot foresee the weather with absolute precision, no one can predict the storms of life. Certainly, we may understand that when someone heads down a destructive path, the outcome won't be good. But for the most part, the trials that really knock us off our feet are the ones we had no idea were on the horizon: a sudden death; an unexpected financial or economic downturn; a devastating medical diagnosis; a violent attack; an earthquake, tsunami, avalanche, or wildfire; and, yes, even weather events such as tornadoes and hurricanes that appear from nowhere and destroy everything.

You don't know when they'll happen, but you *can* be prepared. Jesus promised you so in His Sermon on the Mount. Do you long to know how to persevere no matter what storm rages against you? Do you want to know how to build your life on the right foundation and with the design and materials that will endure? Do you yearn to be so thoroughly convinced of God's work in your life that you can stand strong—regardless of the challenges or consequences?

Do you want to be able to say at the end of it all, like the apostle Paul, "I have fought the good fight, I have finished the course, I have kept the faith" (2 Tim. 4:7)?

Do you long to know how to persevere no matter what storm rages against you?

If this is what you long for, friend, keep reading. Take this challenge to examine what you believe and how you are building your life.

At the back of this book, you'll find some lined pages where you can jot down notes as you read: scriptures that touch your heart, struggles you're going through, convictions you want to become embedded in your heart and soul. These pages are for your personal use.

Choose to stand strong by establishing your life on God Almighty. Because if you do, I'm certain you will stand strong and will not be disappointed (Rom. 10:11).

Part 1

BUILT ON

*No man can lay a foundation other
than the one which is laid, which is Jesus Christ.*

—1 Corinthians 3:11

2

YOUR CONVICTIONS ABOUT THE BIBLE

Good Book or Revelation of the Living God?

It may surprise you that we begin our discussion of standing strong with how we view Scripture. However, when a doctor wants to heal a person of an illness, he knows that treating symptoms is not enough. He must uncover the underlying condition that caused the symptoms and cure it. The same is true when we want to understand why our lives are weak. We cannot look only at the symptoms of a crumbling foundation; we must get at the cause.

DISCERNING RIGHT FROM WRONG

When we go back to the very beginning, we see that it was our own understanding that first separated us from the Lord and set us on the road to defeat. Let me explain.

If you recall in Genesis, God walked with Adam and Eve in

the cool of the day, patiently and wisely teaching them. Of course, good teachers understand how best to instruct their students—how much their pupils can learn in each lesson and how to organize the information in a manner they can comprehend. Knowing God's awesome character and ability, we can certainly assume that He masterfully educated Adam and Eve with great thoughtfulness, wisdom, detail, and care.

But what happened to Adam and Eve? You know that the Lord instructed them not to eat from a certain tree in the Garden of Eden. "The Lord God commanded the man, saying, 'From any tree of the garden you may eat freely; but from the tree of the knowledge of good and evil you shall not eat, for in the day that you eat from it you will surely die'" (Gen. 2:16–17). Soon thereafter, the serpent came to tempt them, saying, "You surely will not die! For God knows that in the day you eat from it your eyes will be opened, and you will be like God, knowing good and evil" (Gen. 3:4–5).

In other words, the serpent promised Adam and Eve that they could know all God knows without having to go to Him to learn it. And that sounded good to them. So when they ate from the Tree of the Knowledge of Good and Evil, Adam and Eve received a mass of information that they were unequipped to handle. The distinctions between good and evil were all meshed together in their minds. Oh, there were concepts that they comprehended as moral and immoral from the beginning—such as the need for God and that acts such as murder and stealing were wicked (Rom. 1:18–25). But because their sin caused them to die spiritually, they lost the capacity to discern right from wrong as they would have learned if they had allowed the Father to teach them. Sadly, as their descendants, the same is true for us (Rom. 5:12–14).

This is why we are prone to sin and why Proverbs 14:12 and 16:25 testify, "There is a way which seems right to a man, but its end is the way of death." Without God, good and evil—life and death—are muddled in our understanding. This is the confusion and anxiety you and I may feel when we face decisions. We want to know the right path to take, but the conflicts of facts and emotions confuse us, making the way unclear.

The serpent promised Adam and Eve that they could know all God knows without having to go to Him to learn it.

This leads us to the first reason we start with the Bible, which is so we can think as God thinks—so we can discern right from wrong.

This is why the Father gave us His Word in the first place (Deut. 6). This is also why He sends His Holy Spirit to guide us when we accept Jesus as our Savior (Heb. 10:15–16). The Holy Spirit teaches us how to think as God thinks. He organizes the truth in a comprehensible way so that we can walk in the manner He designed for us. This is also why Proverbs 9:10 proclaims, "The fear of the Lord is the beginning of wisdom, and the knowledge of the Holy One is understanding." It all begins and ends with Him. We will always be tempted to think that we can know all God knows without having to go to Him to learn it. And we will always be wrong when we do so.

But the beautiful thing about Scripture is that we know it is absolutely true. So much fulfilled prophecy makes it impossible to deny that God's Word is unique and supernatural.

For example, take the Lord's promise to the people of Israel in Ezekiel 36:24. He told them, "I will take you from the nations, gather you from all the lands and bring you into your own land." What nation has ever been reestablished in its land after nineteen centuries of absence? None since the creation of the world. So by all human standards, its fulfillment seemed impossible.

Yet that is exactly what happened with Israel on May 14, 1948, when it was again declared an independent, sovereign state. There is no explanation for it other than the astounding provision of God Almighty and His fulfillment of every promise.

Of course, there is also much archaeological, historical, and textual evidence that the Bible is absolutely trustworthy and reliable. Even non-Christian sources confirm the testimony of Scripture, such as how it reports the interactions of other nations with the people of Israel. We don't have space to go into all of that evidence here, but if you would like to study it further, I discuss it in *Charles Stanley's Handbook for Christian Living*, in the section titled "Inspiration of Scripture."

KNOWING JESUS

Once again, we return to what Jesus said in the Sermon on the Mount: "Everyone who *hears these words of Mine* and acts on them, may be compared to a wise man who built his house on the rock" (Matt. 7:24; emphasis added). So of course we need to go where His words are recorded—to the Bible—to live a strong life.

This is the second reason we need to start with Scripture—because that is where we learn who Jesus really is and what He is teaching us.

Of course, when I talk about learning about Christ through God's Word, I am not talking just about the New Testament—I am referring to the whole counsel of Scripture. There may be those who will claim that the life and words of Jesus are all we ever really need to live the Christian life, and they will limit what Jesus said to the Gospels. But this is actually a faulty understanding of who Jesus is.

In John 1:1 we learn: "In the beginning was the Word, and the Word was with God, and the Word was God." That, of course, is Jesus Himself. He is described as "the Word" and has been revealing Himself from the onset of creation.

Obviously, what is written in the Bible is not the totality of who Jesus is—He is the living God. As the apostle John notes, "There are also many other things which Jesus did, which if they were written in detail, I suppose that even the world itself would not contain the books that would be written" (John 21:25). And John is referring only to what Christ did on earth! Should the entirety of who Jesus is as a member of the Godhead, what He has done, His thoughts, and His ways be fully enumerated, I imagine the whole universe could not house all the volumes. But what we can know for sure is that from Genesis 1:1 to Revelation 22:21, God's character, plan, wisdom, promises, intentions, and purposes are being revealed to us.

As I said, there are those today who question that. Many fail to venture out of the New Testament and into the Old because they feel it is antiquated, difficult to understand, and perhaps even restrictive. Worse, some believers would reduce the totality of Jesus' ministry to the Crucifixion and some practical wisdom about life.

Yes, as Romans 10:9 says, "If you confess with your mouth Jesus as Lord, and believe in your heart that God raised Him from the dead, you will be saved." That is absolutely true—the basis of our salvation is faith in the completed work of Christ on the cross. In fact, the resurrection is our assurance that what He did was sufficient and pleasing to God.

But you can't have a deep, abiding, growing, and intimate relationship with someone if you know only a few things he or she has done. If you don't know a person's purposes, character, ways, what he or she loves and hates, it's impossible to know the person intimately. And how can you testify that "Jesus is Lord" of your life if you don't really know anything about who He is? If you don't have a close relationship with Jesus, how can you be confident that you can really count on Him when the storms of life crash over you? How can you understand the fullness of the hope He offers you?

The basis of our salvation is faith in the completed work of Christ on the cross, and the resurrection is our assurance that what He did was sufficient.

Many Christians continue in a worldly and defeated lifestyle because they've missed the joy and encouragement of discovering how even the smallest details in the Old Testament are brilliantly and gloriously fulfilled in Jesus in a manner that fills the soul with wonder and confidence in Him (John 5:39). When we do see Jesus in the Old Testament, those moments of discovery lead us to realize time and again, "My God is so real, faithful, powerful, wise, and true! There is no way He could possibly let me down!" And even when we experience terrible difficulties, like Job we can say, "I had only heard about You before, but now I have seen You with my own eyes" (Job 42:5 NLT).

28

SO WHERE DO WE GO WRONG?

Of course, you may be thinking, *I love the Word of God and study it, but I still feel defeated. The storms of life have rocked me to the core. And I see people who say they believe the Bible fall every day. It's a great book, but I'm not sure that the Word of God is as powerful as you say.* Sadly, I think many Christians—too many—feel that way.

Central to our problem is *what* we actually believe about the Bible.

If you recall, in the first chapter we talked about Paul, then called Saul, and that he was a Pharisee. Certainly, he was a man who studied Scripture passionately and with great zeal—as the Pharisees were known to do. Yet he missed the very Person all Scripture was pointing to: the Messiah, Jesus. How?

To understand where Saul went wrong in his beliefs, let's look at a famous story from the Talmud (Bava Metzia 59B) that depicts the pharisaical understanding of Scripture. In this story, the rabbis are debating whether a certain kind of oven is clean or unclean. Rabbi Eliezer ben Hyrcanus, one of the most prominent and respected rabbis in the first century, argued that it was clean. The Talmud says,

> On that day, Rabbi Eliezer brought them all sorts of proofs, but they were rejected. Said he to [the other rabbis]: "If the law is as I say, may the carob tree prove it." The carob tree was uprooted from its place a distance of 100 cubits. Others say, 400 cubits. Said they to him: "One cannot prove anything from a carob tree."

Said [Rabbi Eliezer] to them: "If the law is as I say, may the aqueduct prove it." The water in the aqueduct began to flow backwards. Said they to him: "One cannot prove anything from an aqueduct."

Said he to them: "If the law is as I say, then may the walls of the house of study prove it." The walls of the house of study began to cave in. Rabbi Joshua rebuked them, "If Torah scholars are debating a point of Jewish law, what are your qualifications to intervene?" The walls did not fall, in deference to Rabbi Joshua, nor did they straighten up, in deference to Rabbi Eliezer. They still stand there at a slant.

In other words, even though Rabbi Eliezer made all the right arguments and called for three miracles to confirm what he was saying, the other rabbis still wouldn't listen to him. So then Rabbi Eliezer called to the highest authority. The Talmud says,

Said he to them: "If the law is as I say, may it be proven from heaven!" There then issued a heavenly voice which proclaimed: "What do you want of Rabbi Eliezer—the law is as he says . . ."

Rabbi Joshua stood on his feet and said: "'The Torah is not in heaven!' . . . We take no notice of heavenly voices, since You, G-d, have already, at Sinai, written in the Torah to 'follow the majority.'"

Rabbi Nathan subsequently met Elijah the Prophet and asked him: "What did G-d do at that moment?" [Elijah] replied: "He smiled and said: 'My children have triumphed over Me, My children have triumphed over Me.'" (emphasis added)[1]

I wonder if this story is as chilling to you as it is to me. Notice that Rabbi Joshua said, "We take no notice of heavenly voices." The rabbis basically believed that God *had no say in how Scripture was interpreted.* Rather, it was the voice of the majority that would make the decisions as to how to apply Scripture.

Additionally, the rabbis quoted two verses to prove their point: "The Torah is not in heaven" (Deut. 30:12) and "follow the majority" (Exod. 23:2). However, when you look at both of those verses in context, you will see they actually mean the opposite of what the rabbis said they meant. They were wrong in what they believed about the Bible.

First, let's look at the claim that when interpreting Scripture, the rabbis were to "follow the majority" from the command of Exodus 23:2. What the verse actually says is, "*You shall not* follow the masses in doing evil, nor shall you testify in a dispute so as to turn aside after a multitude in order to pervert justice" (emphasis added). In other words, God is saying, "*Don't be* influenced by the majority; do what is right."

Isn't it interesting that even in ancient times, the temptation to be swayed by cultural norms and popular opinions was present? The rabbis fell to that pressure—even going as far as taking Scripture out of context to prove their points. And notice from the story that they went even further and believed they triumphed over God when they did so. But we know that there is no victory in that—quite the opposite. As we noted from Proverbs 14:12 and

16:25, "There is a way which seems right to a man, but its end is the way of death." Destruction is all that awaits us when we fight the living God.

Second, let's look at their absurd assertion that since the Torah is not in heaven, God has no right to interpret Scripture. When we talk about the "Torah," we are specifically referring to the Pentateuch—the first five books of the Bible written by Moses: Genesis, Exodus, Leviticus, Numbers, and Deuteronomy. However, the "Torah" can also refer generally to all the books of the Old Testament. Take your time reading what Moses says in Deuteronomy 30:

Even in ancient times, the temptation to be swayed by cultural norms and popular opinions was present.

"*The Lord your God will bring you* into the land which your fathers possessed, and you shall possess it; and He will prosper you and multiply you more than your fathers. Moreover, *the Lord your God will circumcise your heart* and the heart of your descendants, to love the Lord your God with all your heart and with all your soul, so that you may live . . . *The Lord your God will prosper you* abundantly in all the work of your hand, in the offspring of your body and in the offspring of your cattle and in the produce of your ground, for the Lord will again rejoice over you for good, just as He rejoiced over your fathers; if you obey the Lord your God to keep His commandments and His statutes which are written in this book of the law, if you turn to the Lord your God with all your heart and soul. For this commandment which I command you today is not too difficult for you, nor is it out of reach. It is not in heaven, that you should say, 'Who will go up to heaven for us to get it for us and make us hear it, that we may observe it?' Nor is it beyond the sea, that you should say, 'Who will cross the sea for us to get it for us and make us hear it, that we may observe it?' *But the word is very near you, in your mouth and in your heart, that you may observe it.*" (vv. 5–6, 9–14; emphasis added)

Who would conquer the land and prepare the people's hearts to obey the Lord? God would. Does this exclude the Lord in any way from interpreting the commandments? Of course not. Rather, Moses is saying that in His grace, God would teach them and make everything simple enough to understand and, therefore, to obey. God brought His commandments down to earth, instead of keeping them in heaven, so they would be accessible to you and me.

But the rabbis twisted God's words for their own benefit. Instead of teaching, "This means you can understand Scripture on your own as you walk with the Lord," they insisted, "Everyone must come to us, so we can interpret Scripture for them. Don't go to God—He has nothing to say about this." Sadly, many leaders in the church act the same way.

But with his new understanding of Jesus, the apostle Paul quoted Moses' words here:

The righteousness based on faith speaks as follows: "Do NOT SAY IN YOUR HEART, 'WHO WILL ASCEND INTO HEAVEN?' (that is, to bring Christ down), or 'WHO WILL DESCEND INTO THE ABYSS?' (that is, to bring Christ up from the dead)." But what does it say? "THE WORD IS NEAR

YOU, IN YOUR MOUTH AND IN YOUR HEART"—that is, the word of faith which we are preaching, that if you confess with your mouth Jesus *as* Lord, and believe in your heart that God raised Him from the dead, you will be saved. (Rom. 10:6–9)

In other words, it was not up to us to figure out how to bring Jesus down from heaven or how to resurrect Him from the grave—God planned all of that out for us. In the same way, it is not up to us to decide how to live righteously. He's already thought that out, too. Here's how it works:

First, Jesus was raised from the dead to prove He had given us His righteousness.

Second, when we accept that Jesus is Lord, we then study God's Word and how He has revealed Himself—and as we do, His Holy Spirit shows us how He wants us to grow (Heb. 4:12). We don't make God conform to us and our ideas; rather, we accept Him as our authority. We abandon ourselves to His understanding as our loving heavenly Father (Heb. 12:5–11).

The problem comes when we think like those rabbis—believing that we don't have to take notice of the Lord's heavenly voice. That we know more than God does. That He just laughs when we pick and choose what to obey and what to discard. I can assure you, He does not (Jer. 8:8–12).

Recall what we discussed at the beginning of this chapter about Adam and Eve. It is foolishness to think we can know all God knows without having to go to Him to learn it. Therefore, we must not only honor Scripture but also seek to understand what it means and how we should live by it. We do this by allowing God to speak to us through the *context* and *full counsel* of His Word, rather than just picking and choosing our favorite parts.

GOD'S WORD FIRST

The Bible is the story of God's redeeming love for mankind, and so your convictions about it are supremely important. You will either read the Word and say, "I agree with this, but I don't agree with that," or you will embrace it fully and say, "The Lord God who created the heavens and the earth knows more than I do, and I will trust Him to teach me."

This is the third reason we start with Scripture, which is that every conviction you have proceeds from what you believe about the Bible.

So even before discussing God Himself, we must assess what we think about His Word. Because if you believe the Bible is merely a good book of moral teaching—and not the revelation of the living God— you will not have the reverence and respect for it that you need to build the strong, transformed life you desire. You will base your beliefs about life, the Lord, and all the rest on your own limited wisdom.

> "*The Lord God who created the heavens and the earth knows more than I do, and I will trust Him to teach me.*"

But if you truly believe that the Bible is the inerrant, infallible, eternal Word of the living God and that when you read it the Holy Spirit teaches you how to apply it to your life, then the Lord will work through it to transform you supernaturally. He will reach into the deepest parts of your soul—guiding you in how to live, helping you discern the right path from the wrong, healing your wounds, encouraging you, revealing truth to you that you couldn't have known otherwise, and making your life absolutely rock solid.

Friend, your conviction about Scripture affects all your decisions and way of life. It influences who you become. It determines whether you are able to stand strong.

So make the decision right now.

Will you live by your *preferences?* Will you make choices based on your likes and dislikes and whatever seems best to you in the moment? When making a decision, do you first consider whether it will make you feel good, benefit you, or make you look good to others?

Or will you live by God's Word—His *fixed* principles of conduct and character? Will you navigate your life according to what the Father says and form your beliefs according to what He has revealed in Scripture? Will you take everything you think, believe, and hear and conform it to what the Lord says?

You may be unsure of what to do because of fear. You may believe that if you live by God's Word rather than the standards of society, others won't like you and may even ridicule you. Or perhaps you're afraid that if you live the way God is calling you to live, you will not be as successful at your job as you want to be. Your desire for respect, acceptance, wealth, or significance is on the line, and it would be a great leap for you to choose God over the things that make you feel worthwhile. But friend, don't forget to consider the long-term effects your choices have for you and those you love. If you live merely by preference, you will be like a person speeding down a dark highway with no center line—with no boundaries and in great danger. It will not end well.

This is why we're taught in Romans 12:2, "Do not be conformed to this world"—that is, don't live by the pattern of this age—"but be transformed by the renewing of your mind, so that you may prove what the will of God is, that which is good and acceptable and perfect." The Father wants to give you a new mind and supernatural insight into His thoughts and ways (1 Cor. 2:9–16). He wants to walk with you and show you His awesome will for your life, which is much more meaningful and fulfilling than anything else you could possibly build your life on. You exist for a cause much greater and more important than yourself. You are called to live for Jesus Christ and for His Kingdom, bearing witness to who He is in your life. And when you do, He promises that your joy will be full (John 15:11) and you will bear "fruit that will last" (John 15:16).

So consider carefully: Will you live by your preferences or by God's principles? Will your convictions be wrought from God's Word or from your own imperfect understanding and limited resources? My prayer is that you will live your life based on the unchanging truths found in Scripture and that you'll allow Him to shape what you believe. Because in this way, you'll be able to stand strong no matter what happens.

3

YOUR CONVICTIONS ABOUT GOD, PART 1

The God You Can Know

I have traveled to many countries around the world, and I have found three questions that people consistently have in their hearts, regardless of who they are or where they are from:

1. *Who is the One True God?*
2. *What is He like?*
3. *Can I have a personal relationship with Him?*

People may serve various deities and idols, attend their unique places of worship, and express their religions in very different ways. But deep down inside, there is still an abiding hunger to know who the *real* God is. They want to be certain that the One they're following is the true and Sovereign Creator of heaven and earth. How can they know Him for certain? Is there a way to be sure about who He is and what He desires from us?

These universal questions are understandable when you think about the many religions in the world. In our hearts, we know there is Someone who is beyond us. Romans 1:20 explains, "Since the creation of the world God's invisible qualities—his eternal power and divine nature—have been clearly seen, being understood from what has been made, so that people are without excuse" (NIV). So people inherently know there is some kind of divine power that exists, even if they deny the notion for their own reasons.

But with this being so, how can we be sure we have the *right* ideas about the Lord? It is understandable that those who follow the many false, man-made religions of the world would feel a conflict in their souls. They want to know and experience the One True God, but in their hearts they may sense that their religion provides only an unsatisfactory facsimile of a relationship with Him. As we discussed in the previous chapter, it is impossible to know God unless we go to Him in the way He prescribes.

But this uncertainty doesn't exist only in distant parts of the world. There are people who go to Christian churches every Sunday—people who say they know Jesus as their Savior and worship the God revealed in the Bible—but they are still unsure of who He is. Some doubt Him in an overt way—they cannot tell you who He is, what He is like, or how to have a personal relationship with Him. Others say they know Him well but live in a manner that tells a very different story. They do not honor Him as the One True God because in their hearts they are unsure He really exists. This uncertainty makes for a very weak and insecure foundation for a person's life.

It is impossible to know God unless we go to Him in the way He prescribes.

Of course, you may already have a well-grounded idea of what the Lord is like. Or perhaps, like many people, you have some

40

doubts or misconceptions about His character and what He expects of you. The good news is that once you've made a decision about Scripture, you don't have to make guesses about who God is because He has revealed Himself through His Word—and He will make Himself known to you as you seek Him. He promises in Jeremiah 29:13, "You will seek Me and find Me when you search for Me with all your heart."

THE GOD YOU CAN KNOW

Knowing God was the theme of Paul's message when he spoke to the people in Athens. As many do when arriving in a new place, Paul toured the once great city, which had been the crown jewel of ancient Greece five hundred years prior to his arrival. Although it no longer stood as a great government capital, it was still renowned for its universities and as a philosophical and intellectual center.

Try to picture what Athens must have looked like back in those days when the majestic buildings of the Acropolis still retained their original grandeur, covered with beautiful marble that would have shone in the moonlight. We might imagine the apostle Paul being in awe at the incredible architecture and art.

However, what Paul saw broke his heart.

Acts 17:16 reports that while Paul was waiting for Silas and Timothy, his traveling companions in Athens, "His spirit was being provoked within him as he was observing the city full of idols." He was very agitated because he saw a city of people, wise in their own eyes, who were chasing after false deities that could never save their souls or satisfy their most profound needs. Of course, as we discussed, his Damascus Road experience absolutely transformed Paul's life in a manner he had never imagined possible. He knew that the people of Athens were empty and living in darkness, as he had once been. Oh, they talked and reasoned a great deal about the highest good in life. But by the idols that lined their streets, Paul knew they had no real answers to the deepest questions of their hearts.

So Paul was motivated to proclaim the truth to them. Acts 17:17 tells us, "He was reasoning in the synagogue with the Jews and the God-fearing Gentiles, and in the market place every day with those who happened to be present."

Paul eventually caught the attention of some of the philosophers of Athens, and they were intrigued by what he had to say because he was preaching Jesus and the resurrection. They had never heard anything like that before. So they took him to the Areopagus, also known as Mars Hill—a tremendous ledge of rock located on the northwest side of the Acropolis. In Paul's time, people would often gather there to discuss religion and philosophy and were even known to conduct issues of law there. They asked Paul:

> "May we know what this new teaching is which you are proclaiming? For you are bringing some strange things to our ears; so we want to know what these things mean." (Now all the Athenians and the strangers visiting there used to spend their time in nothing other than telling or hearing something new.) So Paul stood in the midst of the Areopagus and said, "Men of Athens, I observe that you are very religious in all respects. For while I was passing through

and examining the objects of your worship, I also found an altar with this inscription, 'TO AN UNKNOWN GOD.' Therefore what you worship in ignorance, this I proclaim to you." (Acts 17:19–23)

In other words, Paul acknowledged that they were very religious—that they had a sincere hunger for God in their lives. But he also noted that among all the idols they claimed to serve, they still weren't sure they'd found the *real* God. This is why they constructed an altar "to an unknown god"—to the One they'd not yet discovered.

Most likely, they built that altar because they were afraid they would offend a deity they might have missed—especially if they had unwittingly overlooked the actual Lord of all Creation. I believe that whenever we serve anything other than the One True God, we will always sense that something isn't right deep within our hearts—that He is absent. This is true even of believers who have failed to give Him control of a particular area of our lives.

Certainly, the Athenians hadn't found the One who completely filled the longing in their hearts. But Paul had met the Lord Jesus face-to-face, and he could speak with authority on the issue of the One True God. So Paul faithfully introduced them to Him.

> *I believe that whenever we serve anything other than the One True God, we will always sense that something isn't right deep within our hearts—that He is absent.*

Once again, please take your time as you soak in what Paul said. Don't skip over his words trying to get back to mine. Listen to his inspired message:

"The God who made the world and all things in it, since He is Lord of heaven and earth, does not dwell in temples made with hands; nor is He served by human hands, as though He needed anything, since He Himself gives to all people life and breath and all things; and He made from one man every nation of mankind to live on all the face of the earth, having determined their appointed times and the boundaries of their habitation, that they would seek God, if perhaps they might grope for Him and find Him, though He is not far from each one of us; for in Him we live and move and exist, as even some of your own poets have said, 'For we also are His children.' Being then the children of God, we ought not to think that the Divine Nature is like gold or silver or stone, an image formed by the art and thought of man. Therefore having overlooked the times of ignorance, God is now declaring to men that all *people* everywhere should repent, because He has fixed a day in which He will judge the world in righteousness through a Man whom He has appointed, having furnished proof to all men by raising Him from the dead." (Acts 17:24–31)

Paul does an awesome thing here: He gives a step-by-step introduction to the living God—enumerating His attributes, explaining His intentions, and revealing how we can know Him. In other words, Paul answers the three questions:

1. *Who is the One True God?*
2. *What is He like?*
3. *Can I have a personal relationship with Him?*

44

PAUL'S DESCRIPTION OF
THE LIVING GOD

So let's take a look at what Paul says phrase by phrase—because he provides an awesome description of who God is that will help us in standing strong.

"The God who made the world and all things in it" (Acts 17:24).

We see that the One True God—the God you can know—is the Creator of all things. He isn't like those lifeless, powerless idols the Athenians were serving; the people had made those. Rather, He existed before the world began, and He has the unlimited power (omnipotence) and unfathomable wisdom (omniscience) to compose and coordinate every detail of this universe.

This, of course, is always the difference between the One True God and a deity we've created in our minds—the Lord is absolutely unlimited and beyond us, while anything we can imagine is constrained by our own imaginations and somewhat predictable. Be assured, you can absolutely trust God's character, but don't expect to track how He is working in the unseen.

"Since He is Lord of heaven and earth, does not dwell in temples made with hands" (Acts 17:24).

God is absolutely sovereign over everything and is not relegated to one place or another. Although the Greeks and Romans served deities that were supposed to have dominion over certain areas, such as the sea, sky, moon, or underworld, or over particular facets of life, such as the harvest, art, love, war, etc.—the One True

God is omnipresent. He is everywhere at all times and has concurrent dominion over all locations and aspects of life.

However, it is even more accurate to say that *everything is in the Lord's presence*—He is the Ruler of all that exists and He *directs it all* by His mighty power. He is not blind to or shut off from any of it; it all submits to His will and marches to His orders.

"Nor is He served by human hands, as though He needed anything, since He Himself gives to all people life and breath and all things" (Acts 17:25).

This statement is very revealing. Think of the reason we do things for God. We long to win Him over. We want to make Him happy. We yearn to keep Him on our side—as if anything we do for Him or give Him satisfies something within Him. The reality is that whatever we offer Him is like giving a piece of lint to a trillionaire—it is as nothing, because He owns and rules all things. Rather, He has given us our very lives and everything we need.

The Athenians were so busy trying to make God in their own image—ascribing to Him their own standards—that they were blinded to the grandeur of who He really is.

Our God is *already in control,* so He gives us commandments for our good—not because He wants to oppress us. The Lord asks us for sacrifices for our edification—not because He needs anything from us (Ps. 50:10–12). He isn't looking for more possessions; He is revealing whether or not we truly respect Him as God. And as the One who gives us "life and breath and all things," He understands us better than we comprehend ourselves. That's why we seek and serve Him—not to appease Him but because He knows what is absolutely best for us.

"He made from one man every nation of mankind to live on all the face of the earth, having determined their appointed times and the boundaries of their habitation, that they would seek God, if perhaps they might grope for Him and find Him, though He is not far from each one of us" (Acts 17:26–27).

Now, this is interesting. Because, of course, the idols and ideas the Athenians were serving came from all over the known world. And the truth is, if you track the different deities, you can trace them back to their various places of origin. In other words, they come into existence *after* mankind. And the differences between all of them are man-made—according to cultures, geographical distinctions, and regional beliefs.

But with the One True God we can follow humanity back to before our origins and find one unique, identifiable man from whom every other person on earth proceeds. True, other religions purport to have ideas about the beginning. Even science has ascribed the dawn of man to disparate theories. But when we go by Scripture, we know the name of that first man: *Adam.* We know the Creator existed infinite ages before Adam ever came to be, that He formed Adam from the dust of the earth, breathed life into him, and gave him a purpose. Isn't it astounding that we have an account of his life, even though he existed before there was an alphabet to record it? And yet, his story was passed from generation to generation until it came to you and to me. Why? Adam's story not only helps us understand where *we* came from but also demonstrates how deeply God *cared* about Adam. The Lord wanted Adam's story to be known. If that does not fill you with awe, I don't know what will.

Additionally in this passage, Paul seems to say that God

created each one of us with the same forethought and care that He did Adam. We are not accidents—we are each a special creation (Ps. 139:13–14). And our circumstances are not the result of a tragedy or based on a random set of events. On the contrary, they are purposeful, deliberate, and help us realize our profound need for God, so that we "might grope for Him and find Him." So not only do we see that we *can* have a relationship with the One True God, we also realize that He actively creates conditions that prompt us to seek Him. And if God can do all of that, He can certainly reveal Himself to us successfully.

God actively creates conditions that will prompt us to seek Him.

"For in Him we live and move and exist, as even some of your own poets have said, 'For we also are His children.' Being then the children of God, we ought not to think that the Divine Nature is like gold or silver or stone, an image formed by the art and thought of man" (Acts 17:28–29).

I love that Paul sets up this distinction—we are God's children; He is not our creation. He is our Maker and our heavenly Father; we did not invent Him. And so we should come to Him as humble learners rather than as those who already know it all and feel the need to tell Him what to do.

Probably the best illustration of this can be seen if you've ever raised a teenager. Once children enter their teens, they feel the inherent need to express their autonomy and personality. They want to spread their wings and fly. Naturally, as their parent, you understand your child's potential, but you also know their limitations and the areas where they do not yet have sufficient experience to handle the temptations of life. Likewise, you appreciate life on a far more profound level than is possible for someone of a young age. You think about character and morality. You comprehend the importance of resilient relationships, a strong work ethic, fiscal responsibility, sacrificing temporary gain for greater goals, and planning for the future. You know what causes the wounds of life that are so difficult to overcome. You have seen and experienced things that inform how you live, and you want your child to benefit from the wisdom you have gleaned. So as opportunities and challenges arise for your teen, you want to guide him or her successfully through.

Of course, your children see any interference on your part as an obstacle to autonomy and self-expression. They believe you do not understand the pressures they face or how the world now works. You're old—what could you possibly know that they don't? But they do not understand the foundational issues that will so profoundly affect their futures. Their focus is on immediate and temporal needs, not on comprehending that these things could eventually undermine their personhood.

So as a parent, you are left with the constant balance of allowing your children to learn about life on their own, guiding them to make good choices, and protecting them from the traps that would destroy their hopes and prospects. Of course, as our children grow and mature, they begin to realize the wisdom we were trying to impart to them.

The same is true of our relationship with God. Within us is that need to express our autonomy and personality—doubly so, when we get some years on us. And the world is structured around the idea that we must plot our course, live our dreams, strive to succeed, and determine our own destination. We are constantly encouraged to demand our rights and expect what we are due. So we do. But in our self-centered and limited view, we go to the Father like headstrong teenagers—not respecting the fact that He knows more and has a perspective that is more far-reaching than our own. Because no matter how old or experienced we are, we do not have God's supernatural, all-encompassing, and eternal point of view. He has a level of understanding about this life and the life to come that you and I cannot comprehend. Yes, He understands our desire for autonomy; so like a good parent, He balances our need to learn about life on our own with His intent to protect us from the traps that could destroy our future—including the future that begins when life on this earth has ended. And with every challenge, obstacle, pain, heartbreak, trial, joy, and success, He is drawing us, calling us to seek Him.

Now, if you've had a poor family experience, trusting God may seem difficult. We tend to form our understanding of Him based on our experience with our earthly fathers, mothers, or other caregivers. This doesn't give you an excuse to distrust Him; rather, it makes it *all the more important* to seek God with humility and understand who He really is. I lost my own father, Charley Stanley, when I was only nine months old—too young to know what having a dad meant. Later, when I was nine, my mother married John Hall, a very negative, self-centered, and bitter man who did not care for me. That lack of a strong earthly father drove me to seek my heavenly Father, who has never let me down. Therefore, no matter what kind of dad you had, I encourage you to seek God, who is the very best Father you could hope for.

"Therefore having overlooked the times of ignorance, God is now declaring to men that all people everywhere should repent" (Acts 17:30).

God, the good Father that He is, understood that we could never find Him and be restored to Him on our own, so He showed us the way: *repentance.* What is repentance? If you have been in church for any amount of time, you have probably heard that it is a change of mind, a heartfelt sorrow for our sin, which is then followed by a sincere commitment to forsake it and walk in obedience to Christ.

But what is sin? I believe one of the best definitions of it comes from Jeremiah 2:13: "My people have committed two evils: they have forsaken Me, the fountain of living waters, to hew for themselves cisterns, broken cisterns that can hold no water." Cisterns are reservoirs dug into the earth, usually out of solid rock, designed to store water. A fountain, on the other hand, is a natural spring, bubbling up from the earth with an unending supply of fresh, pure water. Think of that in terms of meeting our needs. Instead of choosing God's supernatural, divine, and living water, we often choose to build our own cisterns—meeting our needs in our own way. We reject the ever-flowing spring, which originates in God Himself, for a well of our own creation. Sadly, our ways don't work. They can't. They are inherently broken and fundamentally fall short of the fulfillment we could have if we just committed ourselves to Him.

Sound familiar? Wasn't that exactly what the Athenians were doing—meeting their deep spiritual need for the living God with idols made of wood, stone, and clay? And what did it get them?

Nothing at all. Just a whole bunch of statues that couldn't hear their cries, let alone answer or satisfy them.

And so repentance is deciding to stop trying to meet our own needs in our way and choosing God's way above our own.

Of course, the next natural question is: *How can people who are spiritually dead understand the ways of God, as He expresses Himself and communicates with us through His Holy Spirit?* If you think about it, that's the spiritual equivalent of talking to a corpse.

Repentance is deciding to stop trying to meet our own needs in our way and choosing God's way above our own.

It doesn't matter what you say to a cadaver—it can't hear you. So as we said in the first chapter, God made us spiritually alive through Jesus so that we could receive His Holy Spirit, know Him, follow Him, and be transformed into His likeness. This is the next thing Paul addresses with the Athenians—how we can truly know what is pleasing to God.

"All people everywhere should repent, because He has fixed a day in which He will judge the world in righteousness through a Man whom He has appointed, having furnished proof to all men by raising Him from the dead" (Acts 17:30–31).

Paul explained to the Athenians that the True God had "appointed" a Man who will judge us. God then raised that Man "from the dead" in order to prove to all that He is the One we need to listen to. This Man, of course, is Jesus.

Now please understand, the Athenians had heard the concept of resurrection before. But there are many differences between

Christ's resurrection and those that the other deities were supposed to have experienced.

First, a few of the Greek deities had been said to die and be raised, only to die again. Some were even presumed to be raised on a cyclical basis—dying again and again and each time being raised again. But *none of them* claimed to remain alive *permanently*, as we know Jesus is (1 Cor. 15:3–8; Rev. 1:17–18). Likewise, no other deities promised a bodily resurrection to those who believed in them, as Christ did (Rom. 6:4, 8:11; 1 Cor. 6:14, 15:20–49). They could not guarantee their followers what they did not have themselves.

Second, the resurrections of these idols were never *prophesied in detail* as Jesus' was. Scripture contains thousands of prophecies describing Jesus' First Coming: where He would be born (Micah 5:2); the family He would proceed from (2 Sam. 7:12–13); that He would be born of a virgin (Isa. 7:14); the exact date of His arrival into Jerusalem as *Mashiach Nagid*—our Savior and King (Dan. 9:24–27; Matt. 21:4–11); the details of how He would die (Ps. 22; Isa. 53); and how He would defeat sin and the grave (Ps. 16:10, 22:19–24; Isa. 53:10–12; John 2:19–22), to name only a few. God provided all those details because He wanted us to know with certainty whom we were waiting for.

Third, this also speaks to the fact that *God had a divine, well-thought-out plan that was being fulfilled step-by-step.* The Athenians were accustomed to serving deities who were ruled by their emotions and chaotic in their ways. But the resurrection of Christ was not a spur-of-the-moment decision. It was the marvelous, well-laid provision of the awesome God of Creation who—out of compassion—was readying us for the day of judgment. He is unchanging, reliable, and true—which cannot be said of the idols they served.

Fourth, it is noteworthy that those false deities didn't claim to be the Judge of the world. On the other hand, Jesus understood this as one of His great responsibilities: "Not even the Father judges anyone, but He has given all judgment to the Son" (John 5:22). And because of this immense responsibility, *Jesus came to save us.* It was not His will to condemn us but to provide a way of salvation for us (John 3:17–18; 2 Pet. 3:9). He says:

> "I have come as Light into the world, so that everyone who believes in Me will not remain in darkness. If anyone hears My sayings and does not keep them, I do not judge him; for I did not come to judge the world [referring to the purpose of His First Coming] but to save the world. He who rejects Me and does not receive My sayings, has one who judges him; *the word I spoke is what will judge him at the last day.*" (John 12:46–48; emphasis added)

In other words, Jesus does everything in His power to save us from condemnation. If we reject what He says and the salvation He provided freely on the cross, the condemnation of sin remains on us.

In fact, this is the reason Jesus is worthy of being the Judge of mankind—because only He was *qualified* to pay the heavy price for humanity and only He *succeeded* in paying it. No other can make such a claim.

In Revelation 5:9, it is declared, "Worthy are You to take the book and to break its seals; for You were slain, and purchased for God with Your blood men from every tribe and tongue and people and nation." Only Jesus is merciful enough to judge the world rightly—without prejudice over nationality, race, wealth, or any other distinction. And so, if judgment is to be doled out, it must be by the hand of One who left His throne in heaven, died on the cross in payment for our sins, draws us to His side, and has forgiven us so freely.

And what is the resurrection? Proof that Jesus successfully accomplished it all and that He is who He says He is—the One True God who wants to be known by us.

ANSWERING THE QUESTIONS

So in his brief sermon, Paul answered the three questions that were in the Athenians' hearts:

Who is the One True God? He is the omnipotent, omniscient, and omnipresent Creator of all that is, who existed before time or humanity came into being. He is infinitely beyond us and can never be captured by a work of our hands or even our most profound contemplations (Isa. 55:8–9). He is the authority we should honor and respect above and beyond all others—even our own understanding (Prov. 3:5–6).

What is He like? He is our heavenly Father, who saves us, makes us spiritually alive, cares about us, places us in situations that prompt us to seek Him, heals us, teaches us the way we should go, and disciplines us for our good. He is good and kind, but He is also holy and wise and expects to be respected as the authority He is.

Can I have a personal relationship with Him? Yes. He provides for and seeks out a relationship with you through His Son, Jesus Christ. But you must turn from your attempts at fulfilling your own needs and understanding that He wants what is best for you.

Now, as a believer you know these answers in your mind. But I wonder if you are actively applying these truths about God to every area of your life. I'm not saying that you have to be perfect—none of us is, and we won't be until we see Jesus. But acknowledging who God is is one of the most important keys to standing strong when the trials of life arise. Understanding the character and power of the living God is why Moses could confront Pharaoh and lead the people of Israel out of Egyptian bondage (Exod. 3), why David was able to stand against and triumph over Goliath (1 Sam. 17), and why Elijah had the courage to face the 850 prophets of Ba'al and Ashtoreth (1 Kings 18:20–46).

> *God is good and kind, but He is also holy and wise and expects to be respected as the authority He is.*

Many of us weaken ourselves by deciding there are areas we can never fully entrust to God: personal relationships, finances, business, or what have you. Perhaps your experiences have wounded you in such a way that trusting *anyone* is difficult. It could be that your life feels so out of control that you are grasping for any sense of self-determination. Maybe you have seen things that made you question God because they just don't make any sense to you.

For example, think of the injustices in the world. Because of the great suffering in the world many people have a difficult time believing that God is all-good and all-powerful. If God is omnipotent, loving, and kind, why are children hurt? Why is there so much prejudice and hatred? Why does the abomination of genocide exist? Many conjecture that if the Lord is truly benevolent, then He must be too weak to stop these horrific things from happening. Conversely, they assume that if He is truly omnipotent, then He must not be as loving as Scripture reports. Many people give up on God altogether because they cannot reconcile the differences in their minds. It just does not make any sense to them. And to say we live in a fallen world—well, that doesn't answer all the real and profound questions we have.

However, this all goes back to the fact that God's ways are not our ways and that there are some things He will not reveal to us because His ways are so different from ours (Deut. 29:29; Isa. 55:8–9). However, He will give us wisdom about the challenges we face if we seek Him in faith (James 1:5–6).

There was once a missionary who was called to go to one of the poorest and most difficult parts of the world. No church could grow there because believers were so terribly persecuted. It seemed as if almost as soon as people expressed their trust in Jesus, they were murdered. The persecutors knew that driving out the missionaries was not the answer, because if they killed one, more would come. Instead, their plan was to crush the missionaries' spirits. The basic message was, "If you lead a person to Jesus, we will kill him or her."

So this missionary cried out to God, not understanding why He would call him to such an evil and devastating place. How could he in good faith call people to believe in Jesus if it meant they would certainly be killed for it? Wouldn't that make him complicit in their murder? And why would the Lord call him to a place where he would experience such terrible heartbreak and despair? He was faithful. Why wasn't God blessing him?

One might think the Lord cruel at that point—failing to protect His new believers and putting His willing servant in a hopeless situation. But that assessment judges the circumstances by our own standards and our own limited understanding. It also shows where our focus is. Is it better to protect a person's fifty, sixty, or seventy years on this earth than his or her eternity? Would it have been better for that missionary to leave those people in peace, knowing that they would face a terrible everlasting judgment from which there is no escape (Rev. 20:11–15)? God loved those people enough to send them a witness who could show them the way of salvation through Jesus Christ.

What I mean, friend, is that you have undoubtedly experienced events that seemed incredibly unfair and even cruel. Perhaps you wonder why God didn't protect or provide for you. You may not understand why the Father allowed that deep heartache to wound you as it did. And so, naturally, there are areas of your life from which—whether consciously or unintentionally—you shut Him out. You're not quite sure you can trust Him with certain things if He allowed that heartbreak in your life.

We all have those areas. And usually, we know exactly what they are because that is where we're continually rewounded. And whether we realize it or not, we are like the Athenians, building altars to unknown deities there. We try different things to fill the emptiness, but nothing works. Deep within our hearts, we sense that something isn't right because He is absent from the place we most need to seek Him. The rains batter us, the floods pound against us, and the winds bombard us over and over again—and we fall.

TAKING GOD SERIOUSLY

So what does this have to do with standing strong? Absolutely everything. Some of the trials and obstacles you are experiencing help to bring to the surface the areas where you don't trust God, where you've tried to meet your own needs in your own way, and where you have attempted to mold Him into your own image.

So consider: Is there some sin or area of your life where you repeatedly find yourself saying, "God doesn't really care about that," despite what you have been reading in His Word, understanding in your prayer time, or hearing from the pulpit? Perhaps there is an aspect of your identity in Christ that you have not been able to grasp or some facet of your salvation that doesn't yet make sense to you. Are you undermining yourself by refusing what He is telling you?

Some of the trials and obstacles you are experiencing help to bring to the surface the areas where you don't trust God.

For example, Leviticus 19:16 (NLT) instructs, "Do not spread slanderous gossip among your people," and throughout Scripture, we are admonished to avoid hearsay (Ps. 15:1–3; Prov. 20:19; Rom. 1:29; 1 Tim. 3:11; etc.). Unfortunately, you wouldn't know this if you interact with most church people. Gossip seems to be one of the sins Christians have deemed acceptable, despite what God's Word says. In fact, you might even hear believers spiritualizing gossip by saying they are just sharing prayer requests. But the Lord is clear: Do not participate in spreading rumors.

Now, we know why God commands us not to gossip—doing so can be hurtful to others, may proliferate incorrect information, and ruins our witness. But have you ever considered *why* a person gossips or how it hurts the one who practices it? Sometimes a person talks about other people in order to feel superior to someone he or she envies. An individual may also gossip to feel loved and accepted by others, to experience a connection with others and be included in the buzz. In other words, instead of getting their value and sense of belonging from God, some people do so by spreading speculation about others.

However, their actions accomplish just the opposite of what they're trying to achieve. People who spread secrets and hearsay often lose credibility with those close to them and are frequently hindered in the relationships they really desire. Why? Because you cannot have intimacy with someone who will not be discreet with your deepest feelings. And so people won't disclose their true selves to them. Likewise, studies show that people who gossip usually experience high levels of anxiety because they are so fearful that others will divulge their own faults and failings. Instead of finding worth and acceptance through their actions, they are more isolated than before.

This same thing is true whenever we sin. Instead of achieving what we desire, we find ourselves increasingly empty.

Friend, stop approaching God with the attitude of a head-strong teenager who has it all figured out. Instead, seek your heavenly Father with the understanding that He is your Great and Sovereign Creator—the One who not only set the stars and the heavenly bodies in their places but also coordinates all the cells in your body. He knows how to fill your deepest longing and is worthy of your highest respect and allegiance. So do not fear what He commands you to do. Rather, know for certain that He is always loving toward you—that He knit you in your mother's womb with care and that He is intimately aware of every detail of your life. He will not lead you astray!

Often our difficulty in trusting God is rooted in the tension we see between God's authority and His love.

Some people think the Lord is so lofty and authoritative that they imagine Him as a cold and distant Ruler, moving us about as pawns. His laws seem harsh, and His ways appear strange and uncaring. They obey out of fear rather than reverence.

Others imagine God as so tender that He nods at our sins and failings because He understands we are weak. And because we are His frail children, He doesn't really expect that much from us.

Neither of these caricatures is accurate. Rather, we must hold these two aspects of God's character—His authority and His love—in balance. Yes, His ways are truly higher and more wonderful than we can possibly imagine, and we should always obey Him because He is worthy of our respect and faithfulness. But He is also unconditionally caring toward us—so we can always trust His direction, even when we don't understand it. We can be certain that His most difficult commands are not cold and heartless but given out of His deepest love for us and will ultimately lead to blessings. Yes, obeying Him may sometimes go against our nature and be terribly difficult, but obedience always leads to our ultimate liberty and joy.

With this in mind, I ask you to examine your heart. What is God working in you through the trials you experience? What is it that you fear? What need are you continually attempting to fill? In what way do you always try to protect or prove yourself? What is the stressor that makes you lose your hope in God altogether? The Lord is targeting the area of your heart where you struggle for a reason: He wants you to be free. You've set up an idol there, a likeness of deity that is not the One True God. And He will not compete with it. He will focus on that area until you are willing to acknowledge that your ways have failed and that He is the real and rightful Lord of your life.

Friend, you have the opportunity for an intimate and transformative relationship with the Sovereign Lord of all that exists. I'm not talking only about salvation but also about true fellowship with the living God. *He is the God you can know.* And in the next chapter, we will discuss His awesome provision, which allows you to be close to Him eternally. So set your heart to truly know and honor Him, because when you know that the Sovereign God of Creation is with you and loves you, you will certainly always *stand strong.*

4

YOUR CONVICTIONS ABOUT GOD, PART 2

What Does It Mean to Have a Savior?

The Old Testament is very instructive about who God is:

+ He is *Yahweh*—the existing One and Great I Am.

+ He is *Elohim*—the One who is infinite in power and absolutely faithful to keep His promises to you.

+ He is *El Shaddai*—the Almighty God, the Most High over all, who is always victorious.

+ He is *El Olam*—the Everlasting God, who is from eternity past and will endure infinitely into the future.

+ He is *El Roi*—the God who sees you.

+ He is *Yahweh Rapha*—the One who heals you.

+ He is *Yahweh Rohi*—your Shepherd who guides you.

+ He is *Yahweh Shalom*—your peace.

- He is *Yahweh Yireh*—your great and mighty Provider, the One who perceives your needs and faithfully supplies what will fulfill them.

As beautiful and inspiring as all these descriptions are, they do not fully portray what God is like. They are only pieces of a vague and distant view of Him. In fact, throughout the Old Testament, from the Fall of mankind on, God is separate from the people, represented by specially chosen intermediaries. Faithful men such as Abraham, Joseph, Moses, David, and Nehemiah would go to the Lord on behalf of the people and carry out His purposes. He also raised up prophets and priests to declare His will. Even in the Temple, His glorious presence in the Holy of Holies was obscured by an extremely thick and heavy, multicolored veil. Only the high priest was permitted to pass through it on one day a year—the Day of Atonement (Lev. 16).

To reinforce the reality of our separation, God even tells Moses, "You cannot see My face, for no man can see Me and live!" (Exod. 33:20). So even though Scripture describes the Almighty God as One who provides for and cares for us, the fact that He "dwells in unapproachable light" (1 Tim. 6:16) and we cannot see or touch Him may give us the impression that He is aloof and unfriendly. It is difficult for us to imagine Him as warm, close, and loving when there is so much unknown about Him. It is therefore no wonder that God often feels so distant and removed from us.

A TRUE REPRESENTATION

However, as we discussed previously, Paul told the Athenians, "He is *not* far from each one of us" (Acts 17:27; emphasis added). We understand from the first chapters in Genesis that God's will is to walk with us daily, in intimate fellowship (Gen. 3:8–9). Yet more was needed for us to know Him and be able to embrace Him (Jer. 31:3–34; Ezek. 36:25–27). So Jesus Christ came both *to ready us to receive* God and *to reveal His true nature* to us.

John 1:18 testifies, "No one has seen God at any time; the only begotten God who is in the bosom of the Father, He has explained Him." Jesus is the faithful and trustworthy expression and illumination of who God is because He Himself is God in human flesh. That is, Jesus came to communicate who God is in visible form and in personal terms so that we can comprehend what God is like.

Colossians 1:15 tells us, "He is the image of the invisible God." Likewise, Hebrews 1:3 reports, "He is the radiance of His glory and the exact representation of His nature." Jesus is the authentic, trustworthy representation and revelation of the Father. This is who He was when on this earth, this is who He continues to be today, and this is who He will be forever. As fully God and fully Man, Jesus shows us exactly what an amazing relationship with the Lord can look like. When we read about Jesus healing the sick, comforting the brokenhearted, casting out demons, freeing the bound, and resurrecting the dead, we see an incredible picture of who the Father truly is and how He feels about us. As Jesus Himself said, "He who has seen Me has seen the Father" (John 14:9).

This means that when Jesus willingly and lovingly touches and heals the leper, God Himself is doing so (Matt. 8:2–3). He is compassionate toward us in our very worst infirmities, even the ones that make others uncomfortable or fearful.

When Christ comforted the widow who had lost her son and raised him up again (Luke 7:12–15), it was the Lord of all Creation doing so—giving flesh to the promise, "The Lord is near to the brokenhearted and saves those who are crushed in spirit" (Ps. 34:18).

As fully God and fully Man, Jesus shows us exactly what an amazing relationship with the Lord can look like.

Not only can we now look into His face, but God looks into our faces with love, power, mercy, and commitment even in our most heartbreaking failings—just as Jesus did with the woman who was caught in the act of adultery. Yet as he commanded this woman, He also commands us to "sin no more" (John 8:11). He longs to see us free from the heartache, emptiness, and shame sin has brought upon us. Jesus came to reveal God to us in a real, meaningful, and tangible way.

READYING US FOR RELATIONSHIP

Now, please understand, this doesn't mean we no longer need the Old Testament. The revelation of Christ in the New Testament sheds light on the mysteries of the Old Testament, and the Old Testament adds profound meaning to the truth found in the New Testament. They are together one beautifully crafted and progressive unveiling of the Lord's character and plan.

In fact, it is in the Old Testament that we read that we need God to be *Yahweh Tsidkenu*—our righteousness—and that He would become our righteousness through the line of David. Jeremiah 23:5–6 teaches, "'Behold, the days are coming,' declares the Lord, 'When I will raise up for David a righteous Branch; and He will reign as king and act wisely and do justice and righteousness in the land. In His days Judah will be saved, and Israel will dwell securely; and this is His name by which He will be called, "The Lord our righteousness."'"

Of course, we understand the "Branch" to be Jesus. Our holy God had to confer His own righteousness upon us because His justice requires payment for every sin. Yet nothing we could do on our own would ever be enough to pay our sin debt in full.

We know this from the Old Testament sacrificial system, when priests would make daily offerings for the nation's transgressions (Exod. 29:38–39). People also brought sacrifices of lambs and other animals to the Temple as payment for their iniquities (Lev. 5:5–7). These offerings were repeated day after day in an unending cycle. Yet an animal's blood could never truly take away sin—it could only cover it (Heb. 10:3–4).

So one Man—the virgin-born, sinless, incarnate Son of God—voluntarily offered Himself to stand in our place and receive the judgment for our sin. And when the blameless Lamb of God laid down His life as a substitute for all men, payment for sin was complete, sufficient, and accepted. Jesus bore in His body the full penalty for our disobedience—past, present, and future (1 Pet. 2:24). No further sacrifice is required (Heb. 7:27). That is why when Jesus died on the cross, the immense veil that separated all men from the holiest place in the Temple tore in two (Matt. 27:51; Mark 15:38; Luke 23:45). God showed that He had removed the barrier between Himself and us (Heb. 6:19–20, 10:19–20; 2 Cor. 3:16).

And the fact that it was ripped from top to bottom signified that the Lord, not man, had removed what separated us.

So when we receive Jesus as our personal Savior, we no longer bear the penalty of our transgressions. We are proclaimed "not guilty" *forever* because He took our place. As we discussed in the previous chapter, when we receive His gift by faith, we are also made spiritually alive by His sacrifice, which means we can have a deep and meaningful relationship with the Lord.

THE IMPORTANCE OF INTIMACY

Although having a personal relationship with God is something we often talk about, I wonder if we truly understand what has been given to us. Our greatest need as people is to know that we are loved, respected, valued, accepted, and secure. We want to know for certain that someone cares for us. This need motivates us in untold ways. We want to achieve great things so we can feel worthwhile. We strive to prove that we are worthy of other people's admiration. Or perhaps we hide parts of ourselves in order to diminish the pain of loneliness and isolation, but only succeed in increasing it. Whether we wish to admit it or not, we are endeavoring to fill these profound internal needs in ways that ultimately don't work.

I have often said, "Our intimacy with God, His highest priority for our lives, determines the impact of our lives." Why does the Lord deem intimacy so important? Because it is only through such a close relationship with Him that our inscrutable needs are truly met. He created us, knows everything about us, and always does

68

what is best for each of us—every time and in every situation. And whether we realize it or not, there is a longing within each of us to know God and be known by Him. This happens on a level within us that is untouched by human comprehension or earthly substitutions. It is the yearning we talked about in the last chapter, which led the Athenians to build the altar to the unknown god. Yet the Lord God is not merely the object of our search—from Him flows all that is lacking in us and what can be possible through us.

Not only is our intimacy with God important for us personally due to our own basic need, but the full potential of our lives can be reached *only* through a relationship with Him. Our lives were made to be earthen vessels that shine forth His glory (2 Cor. 4:7). And the more we know God, the more He lives His life through us, giving us His power and revealing His plan for us. That is why it is only through our intimacy with God that our needs are truly fulfilled and we can stand strong.

THE INVITATION TO INTIMACY

As our Savior, Jesus *prepares* us and *invites* us to engage in intimacy with God. But first, before we go any further, I would like to take a moment to explain what I mean by *intimacy*. Whenever I talk about intimacy, some people immediately think of sexual interaction—what we can see, touch, and feel. Although I am referring to the relationship between two individuals, what I'm referring to is much deeper than just physical closeness. You can be geographically or physically close to another person for years and yet not really know him or her at all.

Rather, I am referring to the closeness of a relationship that impacts and exposes who you are as a person at the deepest levels. It is the kind of interaction that reaches into your most private thoughts and issues of identity and exposes the most difficult places in a manner that is redemptive and healing. One could say it is "into-me-see." When you get that close to someone, you tend to learn a lot about yourself because you see yourself through his or her eyes. You realize that you were created for more than what you're living for, and you gain the courage to go after it. In other words, a truly intimate relationship is healing, revealing, and motivating—bringing out the very best in you.

Of course, you may wonder: *How can I know for sure that God wants that kind of relationship with me?*

To answer this, I invite you to consider how the Lord created you. He formed you in His image and likeness—with intellect, emotions, and a will that provides a platform from which you can relate to Him. What other creature exhibits such a capacity or has been given such an honor? He created you in such a manner for one reason—so you could know Him in the deepest parts of your being, personally and intimately.

Likewise, remember that before salvation, you were spiritually dead. You did not and could not seek the Lord on your own. Romans 3:11 affirms, "There is none who understands, there is none who seeks for God." Without the ability to commune with the Father *spiritually*, you cannot truly know Him.

This is why Jesus said, "No one can come to Me unless the Father who sent Me draws him" (John 6:44). In every instance throughout Scripture, God is the one who takes the initiative in the relationship between Himself and humanity *because only He has the power and ability to bridge the spiritual gap that is between us.*

This is the very reason Christ made such a costly sacrifice to save you. If God did not truly want an intimate relationship with you, He would not have paid such a lofty price.

So when you feel that deep desire to know God, understand that He is drawing you to Himself.

In every instance, God is the one who takes the initiative in the relationship between Himself and humanity because only He has the power and ability to bridge the spiritual gap that is between us.

And He is, without a doubt, calling you to deep fellowship with Himself in order to bring out the very best in you.

THE WHY?

Why? Why has God gone through all this trouble to relate to us? As we've noted, the Lord doesn't need us in any way, not even to fill loneliness. From eternity, the Father has been in perfect, undividable, divine fellowship with the other two Persons of the Godhead—the Son, Jesus, and the Holy Spirit. No fellowship could be more fulfilling. And as we saw in Acts 17:24–25 (NLT), "He is the God who made the world and everything in it . . . human hands can't serve His needs—for He has no needs. He himself gives life and breath to everything, and He satisfies every need." If this is the case, why did He create us? Why does He pursue us?

I believe we can find the answer in Revelation 4:11: "Worthy are You, our Lord and our God, to receive glory and honor and power; for You created all things, and *because of Your will they existed, and were created.*" The King James Version translates it this way: "For Thy *pleasure* they are and were created." In other words, the Lord created us because it gave Him joy to do so. Also, from 1 John 4, we know that "Love is from God" (v. 7) and "God is love" (v. 16). True, unconditional love always expresses itself. In fact, we are told, "By this the love of God was manifested in us, that God has sent His only begotten Son into the world so that we might live through Him" (v. 9). The Lord created and saved us so He could actively express His love to us.

Let's look more directly at why God *created* us and why He went to so much trouble to *redeem* us through the death of His Son and then *pursue* an intimate relationship with us. Two reasons come to mind: He created us, as we've said, so He could express His love. But He also created us so that He could accomplish His work through us.

First, we are the objects of God's love. He expresses His love and character to you.

Friend, the Lord didn't save you just so He could have another follower, so He could number you on the church rolls and see you dressed nicely on Sundays. Rather, He wants you to know Him and experience how deeply He cares for you. He is your Creator, the One who looks at you with tenderness and joy. And He longs for you to trust Him as an intimate Friend—as the One who walks with you on the mountains of success and in the valley experiences of life. He wants you to understand His ways—how He works in the world and the detailed manner in which He is watching over you. He wants you to sense how deeply He loves you so you can feel the joy and purpose you were created for. So He engineers circumstances where you can experience His attributes at work on your behalf.

Think about the times you have been in a trial and absolutely could not help yourself. Maybe you are facing such a challenge now. The Lord wants you to draw near to Him and experience His almighty, all-encompassing power poured out for you so you can realize how *completely* you can depend on Him. So you can know that He is not just the Savior of your soul but also your Defender and Deliverer in every moment of your life. In such times, we can picture Him as a Dad standing in the swimming pool, calling out to his child, "Jump! I'll catch you! You can do it!" The Lord wants you to know that you are always safe when you rely upon Him. He wants you to embrace the freedom and joy of knowing that His everlasting arms are outstretched to catch you as you obey Him.

This was certainly the case for Gideon. God called upon Gideon to stand against the immense invading armies of the Midianites. However, being from the smallest, weakest tribe, Gideon felt too feeble and ill-equipped for the challenge. The Lord's answer? "Surely I will be with you" (Judg. 6:16). In fact, God wanted Gideon to be absolutely certain that He was the One—the only One—delivering him. So the Lord said to Gideon, "The people who are with you are too many for Me to give Midian into their hands, for Israel would become boastful, saying, 'My own power has delivered me'" (Judg. 7:2). And through a process of elimination, He reduced Gideon's ranks from twenty-two thousand to three hundred soldiers. Ultimately, God sent a terrifying dream to the Midianites, which frightened them so much that they turned their swords on each other. In this way, God gave Gideon the victory (Judg. 7:12–15). The Lord delivered Israel in a manner that Gideon could never have foreseen or engineered on his own.

Consider that in terms of your own battles today. It could be that not only is the challenge too big for you to begin with, but you feel as if you've been cut off from the resources you're accustomed to relying upon. You are more limited, weak, and powerless than ever, and you cannot figure out why the Father would allow that to happen to you. Stand by, friend. Your omnipotent God is orchestrating your deliverance in a manner you could never have imagined so that you can see the mighty workings of His power on your behalf.

When we experience difficulties, our first consideration is often how we feel about it or what we could lose. But do you realize the difference it could make in your life if your first thought was about God? That's what I always ask when some trial arises: "Lord, what are You up to? What do You want me to learn from this?" Because I know that nothing touches my life without His first allowing it.

Your omnipotent God is orchestrating your deliverance in a manner you could never have imagined so that you can see the mighty workings of His power on your behalf.

Think of the assurance Jesus gives us as His followers: "I give eternal life to them, and they will never perish; and no one will snatch them out of My hand" (John 10:28). We rest in the palm of His hand. Yes, this speaks to our eternal security. However, it also speaks to our lives as a whole as we are safely garrisoned about by His mighty hand. So *anything* that comes to us must first make it past Him. And since nothing in all creation can move even the Lord's finger, anything He *permits* must ultimately be for His greater purposes (Rom. 8:28–29). And, of course, as we just said, God's first reason for pursuing an intimate relationship with you is to express His love and character to you. So when you experience circumstances that you don't understand, watch for what the Lord is trying to teach you about Himself.

Second, God redeems and pursues us to accomplish His work through us.

You were formed in your mother's womb with the express purpose and ability to exalt the Lord in a unique way that would draw people to Him. We know this from Isaiah 43:7. The Lord says, "Bring all who claim me as their God, for I have made them for my glory. It was I who created them" (NLT).

Now, we might think that God created us because He needs to be praised. But remember that Jesus said, "I tell you, if these [people] become silent, the stones will cry out!" (Luke 19:40). God does not need people who will praise Him, because all creation already worships Him (1 Chron. 29:11). However, you and I require purpose in our lives—we need to feel useful and wanted. To feel like our life means something in a way that endures. So the Father invites us to become part of His redemptive work in the world—not just for our sakes but also on behalf of the people He will reach through us. When we do this, we experience at least the following five blessings.

1. *First, when God accomplishes His work through you, you find significance.* Think about it: The God who created you knows *why* He made you. Ephesians 2:10 explains, "We are His workmanship, created in Christ Jesus for good works, which God prepared beforehand so that we would walk in them." He knows what assignments He has given you, and

He actively prepares you for them so that you can succeed. And as you fulfill the roles He created you for, you feel most valued and respected.

2. *As God accomplishes His work through you, your life is filled with peace.* When you are not walking *in* God's will, you are walking *outside* it, and that will naturally cause static in your relationship with Him—the pain of walking *against* His purposes. But when you are accomplishing the work He planned in advance for you to do, you will feel a harmony with God and a tranquility in life that surpasses anything this world can offer.

3. *Likewise, when God accomplishes His work through you, you are filled with joy.* There is no more profound happiness in this life than to feel the Lord's pleasure. When you are accomplishing His work, with His Holy Spirit enabling and empowering you, knowing you are fulfilling the purposes for which He created you—that is life at its best. You feel God's power flowing through you and His joy in your obedience. It is as if the outpouring of your life becomes a worship service to Him. There is nothing in this world better than that.

4. *As God accomplishes His purposes through you, eternal fruit is produced.* In John 15:16, Jesus says, "You did not choose me, but I chose you and appointed you so that you might go and bear fruit—*fruit that will last*" (NIV; emphasis added). Think about that. Every one of us knows the pain of working hard to build something up, only to have someone else tear it down. But Jesus promises that what He achieves through

you will last *forever*. Why? Because He makes you into a "fisher of men" (Matt. 4:19). You are influencing others in an indestructible way that makes a difference to them *in eternity*.

5. *Finally, God's work accomplished in you impacts others after you are gone.* Philippians 1:6 assures you that "He who began a good work in you will perfect it until the day of Christ Jesus." What you do in obedience to God will continue having an exponential influence in other people's lives long after you have passed away. We can see this in nature. If you have ever done any gardening, you know that certain plants are *annuals*—you must replant them every year because they have a limited life cycle. But there are also *perennials*, plants that don't just endure from year to year but also grow and propagate. So, for example, let's say you plant a perennial—such as a hosta, liriope, daylily, or what have you—during one growing season, and by the next, it has multiplied, producing three more plants. You divide those three out and replant them. The year after that, you find that not only has the original perennial produced three more plants, but its offspring have yielded three each as well. So in two growing seasons, you have gone from one perennial to sixteen. If those sixteen all generate three plants each, the next year you will find sixty-four in your garden. So even when the original perennial eventually dies, it will continue to bear fruit through its offspring. This is a principle of the Christian life—your life continues to exert influence even after you are gone, because Jesus, who began the work in you, continues to make it flourish.

GROWING IN INTIMACY WITH GOD

So consider the existence we've just discussed—a life based on a love relationship with the living God and that faithfully cooperates with Him as He accomplishes His work in us and through us. This life is filled with significance, peace, and joy; it bears fruit in eternity; it has an enduring impact in this world. To me, that all adds up to a strong life—a person who is not easily shaken by the storm winds.

Your life continues to exert influence even after you are gone, because Jesus, who began the work in you, continues to make it flourish.

And if Jesus—God incarnate—gave His life so that we could be saved and experience a profound relationship with Him, shouldn't we be willing to pursue what He offers us? Shouldn't we strive for the deepest, most meaningful interaction with the living God our hearts can experience, knowing that a strong life is the result?

Of course, the answer is yes. But the tragedy is that most believers never realize what God has provided for them or can do in their lives. They think salvation is the beginning and the end of the road—or at least the major part of it. Yet Jesus was clear: "I came that they may have life, and have it *abundantly*" (John 10:10; emphasis added). Not a weak life. Not an existence that is continually torn down by the storms of life. Rather, an extraordinary life—an existence characterized by the supernatural indwelling of the living God that triumphs no matter what winds or waves rage against it.

So, what is the process for growing in intimacy with God?

You may have been asking the above question. *How can I*

become more intimate with Him? How can I really experience that abundant life?

The key to intimacy with God is to respond to Him in faith. You see, once we are saved, the Lord begins to reveal Himself to us and challenges us to trust Him. A first step, for example, is choosing to be baptized. Baptism is not necessary for salvation, of course. But it is a public declaration of identification with Jesus that symbolizes His life, death, and resurrection (Rom. 6:3–4). It is an act of obedience—an outward expression of your inward commitment to follow Christ and live for Him.

The Christian life is full of such choices. Through His Word and through prayer, God will reveal issues in you He wants to deal with—behavior that needs to be changed or deeper commitments He wants you to make. You will either respond to Him in faith, which will allow Him to work in your life, or you won't. You will either turn from your ways and trust Him, actively declaring Him to be Lord of your life, or you'll continue trying to be in charge. But be warned: If you insist on keeping the control, you will remain stuck at that level in your relationship with God. That's not the abundant life—that's a house headed for a fall (Matt. 7:26–27).

This is the nature of a relationship with the Lord and how we grow in intimacy with Him. God reveals Himself to us and we respond in faith. It happens again and again because it is a process that builds on itself. Jesus said it like this: "He who has My commandments and keeps them is the one who loves Me; and he who loves Me will be loved by My Father, and I will love him *and will disclose Myself to him*" (John 14:21; emphasis added). Do you see the incredible promise He makes? As you trust Him enough to obey Him, He reveals more of Himself to you.

This is important because of the principle we find in 1 Corinthians 2:

> "No eye has seen, no ear has heard, and no mind has imagined what God has prepared for those who love Him." But it was to us that God revealed these things by His Spirit. For His Spirit searches out everything and shows us God's deep secrets. People who aren't spiritual can't receive these truths from God's Spirit. It all sounds foolish to them and they can't understand it, for only those who are spiritual can understand what the Spirit means. Those who are spiritual can evaluate all things . . . We understand these things, for we have the mind of Christ. (9–10, 14–16 NLT)

In other words, when God reveals Himself and we trust Him by obeying, *it is as if we are allowing the very mind of Christ to be set free in us.* We catch glimpses of the incredible things the Father has planned for us. We better understand His thoughts and plans, and we receive His wisdom.

When God reveals Himself and we trust Him by obeying, it is as if we are allowing the very mind of Christ to be set free in us.

Remember how God walked with Adam and Eve in the cool of the day? What an incredible privilege they had to know Him and fellowship with Him face-to-face. Yet, as believers, every time the Lord discloses Himself to us and we respond in faith, we have the exact same privilege. We have the Spirit of the living God and the mind of Christ guiding us.

Now, I said it is through God's Word and through prayer that the Father will reveal issues He wants to deal with in you. We've discussed the importance of Scripture, and will explore prayer in the following chapter. However, it is crucial that we understand that intimacy with the Father is more than the mechanical acts of reading Scripture, prayer, worship, doing ministry, or sharing our faith. These are great things. But we can get so busy doing things *for* God that we forget to relate *to* Him.

The depths of intimacy go beyond these activities. This is why Jesus made that shocking statement in Matthew 7:22–23: "Many will say to Me on that day, 'Lord, Lord, did we not prophesy in Your name, and in Your name cast out demons, and in Your name perform many miracles?' And then I will declare to them, 'I never knew you; depart from Me, you who practice lawlessness.'"

A relationship with God is not about doing good works or earning your way to salvation. We have a relationship with Him in order to *know* Him. We aren't checking off boxes on a to-do list so we can call ourselves "good Christians" or feel like we've paid our dues (Hosea 6:6). Rather, we read Scripture and pray so we can discover more about Him, hear His voice, and understand His ways. We are obedient to the Lord out of our gratefulness to and respect for Him.

This is the kind of intimate relationship you see with the true saints of God—with Moses, David, Paul, and all the others. But you may still be wondering . . .

Does God really offer this kind of intimacy to me?

Can I really experience the same fellowship with God that Abraham had? Can I talk to Him as a friend like Moses did? (Exod. 33:11).

Absolutely you can! Just because there are no more burning bushes and God hasn't called anyone to part the Red Sea in quite a while doesn't mean we can no longer have the depth of interaction with Him they did. The Father's desire is for you to have a relationship with Him that is as close as possible. God has purposed to reproduce His life in and through your life. In order for that to happen, He must reveal Himself to you and bring you into an intimate relationship with Himself.

Think of that! You can have God's very life flowing through you!

Think of that! You can have God's very life flowing through you!

He is ready to develop that relationship with you, but it is dependent on your willingness.

THE BARRIERS TO INTIMACY

With all the possibilities we've discussed, you may be wondering, *Why don't all believers have this relationship with Him?* I find that there are three major barriers to our intimacy with God.

1. *Fear.* Some people are afraid of facing the truth about themselves, and others are fearful of the requirements God may demand of them. Be assured, the Lord wants you to be free. But sometimes it is very difficult to relinquish the things that give you a false sense of security. When people are fearful of giving up their strongholds, they will be tempted to avoid God so they will not be accountable for the truth He reveals to them.

2. *Pride.* This is an overemphasis on self. In our modern world as believers, we are more likely to worship our own opinions than an idol made of wood or stone. In essence, we

believe we know better than the Lord does, and we refuse to honor and respect Him as God. This is why pride is an abomination to Him (Prov. 8:13). We can demonstrate pride in overt ways such as outright rejecting God, willful disobedience or rebellion, and boastfulness. Or we can do so in subtle ways such as avoiding time alone with Him, being unwilling to admit our need for Him in a certain area, or doing all the talking when we pray to Him.

3. *Busyness.* The key to an intimate relationship with the Father is our time alone with Him, so when we hurry through it because of busyness, we're truly missing out. Of course, there are many people—especially religious leaders— who can say, "I spend a lot of time in God's Word." But I am not talking about time looking for a sermon, a Sunday school lesson, or a verse to make you feel better. This is not just picking and choosing what you like or what you can say to others. Too many believers spend time in God's Word but never actually allow its Author to reveal Himself or transform them through it. Friend, don't do that. Take the time to know God *intimately.* Make Him your priority, and every other responsibility will certainly fall into place.

Unfortunately, the result of fear, pride, and busyness is that many Christians don't experience true intimacy with God. Instead, we allow this world to motivate our actions and choke Him out of the areas where we really need Him, choosing instead to submit to popular opinion and culture. We compartmentalize the Lord, allowing Him to occupy only a small portion of our existence.

But in John 8:32, Jesus teaches, "You are from below, I am

from above; you are of this world, I am not of this world." In other words, the unsaved are of a different nature from Christ. They are of this world—they belong to it, act according to its rules, and are enslaved to its ways (Rom. 6:12–16).

But Jesus is different. He is from above. So as we grow spiritually, we should be leaving our worldly ways behind us—taking on Jesus' likeness, image, and character (Rom. 8:29). Likewise, as our closeness and identification with God grow, our attachment and allegiance to the world and its ways must consequently decrease. The two relationships are mutually exclusive.

As we saw in the previous chapter, when we prioritize anything over our relationship with the Lord, He sees it as competition and will target whatever comes between us and Him. We see this throughout the Old Testament with all of the idolatry the Israelites committed.

If you recall, once the Lord had freed Israel from bondage and slavery in Egypt, He led them to Mount Sinai and told them through Moses: "You shall have no other gods before Me. You shall not make for yourself an idol, or any likeness of what is in heaven above or on the earth beneath or in the water under the earth. You shall not worship them or serve them; for I, the Lord your God, am a jealous God" (Exod. 20:3–5).

Of course, the Egyptians were accustomed to serving multiple deities—just like the Athenians we studied in the previous chapter. But the Lord was calling His people, Israel, to a new way.

But while they were encamped around Sinai, they became disheartened because Moses was taking a long time coming down from the mountain where he was receiving God's direction. So the people told Aaron, "Come, make us a god who will go before us;

as for this Moses, the man who brought us up from the land of Egypt, we do not know what has become of him" (Exod. 32:1). In other words, they thought Moses was gone, so they were seeking an idol for *guidance.*

Sadly, this wasn't the only time the Israelites went looking for other deities. Once they settled in the Promised Land, they often sought the storm deity of the Canaanites named Ba'al (Jer. 11:17). He is usually depicted holding a lightning bolt because he was thought to defeat enemies and produce crops. So their attraction to Ba'al was based on their desires for *security* and *prosperity.*

Guidance, security, and *prosperity*—the three areas that often make us fall as well. We are often afraid to let go of these three facets of our lives, and we may arrogantly believe we know more in these areas of life than the One who created us.

Whenever the Israelites would seek one of these false deities, the Lord would send situations to humble His people so they would seek

We may arrogantly believe we know more about life than the One who created us.

Him and choose His ways. And just like the Israelites, He may allow us to experience brokenness so that we turn back to Him.

OVERCOMING THE BARRIERS

So friend, I ask you to examine your heart. Jesus is the Savior of your soul, but have you really made Him the Redeemer, Defender, and Deliverer of every part of your life? Do you truly desire to have an intimate relationship with Him—or are fear, pride, and busyness holding you back?

I've said it often throughout this book, because it is the truth: *The trials you are experiencing are in your life for a purpose.* The Lord is showing you where you are clinging to forms of guidance, security, and prosperity that are from below—where the foundation of your life is cracked and faulty. He wants you to let go of them so He can have first place in your life and raise you up to the highest, best, and strongest your life can be.

So as you think about the challenge you are currently facing, prayerfully ask yourself:

- *Am I being reverent?* Am I respecting who God is and that He knows better than I do (Ps. 25:12)? Or am I seeking something else for my guidance, security, and prosperity?

- *Do I really love God?* Or am I serving Him out of obligation (Hosea 6:6)?

- *Am I being transparent in my times alone with Him?* Am I exposing my whole heart to Him and giving Him access to every area of my life?

- *Am I being honest with Him about my sinfulness?* Am I allowing Him to free me from it, or am I covering it over with excuses and denials?

- *Am I truly willing to eliminate the barriers that separate me from God?*

- *Do I really trust God?* Am I willing to accept that His plans are truly best for me? Do I have faith to walk with Him even when I don't understand how He is leading me (Prov. 3:5–6)?

+ *Am I willing to embrace disciplines that promote intimacy with God*—not to win His favor or to make myself look good but to know Him as intimately as I can?

+ *Am I truly taking the time I need to meditate on God's Word?* Do I not only read Scripture but also think about it and learn more about Him?

+ *Am I listening for God's voice?* Am I watching for how He is moving in my life?

+ *Am I teachable?* Am I open to His instruction and direction (Ps. 25:4–5)?

+ *Have I surrendered my life to Him?* Do I understand that as my Creator, He knows what I was formed to do and what will bring true fulfillment to my life?

Allow God to speak to you as you consider each of these questions. Write down what He tells you and don't ignore anything that comes to mind. God wants to overcome every barrier, stronghold, and place of bondage in your life. So let Him lead you not only to profound intimacy but also to freedom.

AFTER HIS HEART

So friend . . .

+ if you want to be loved and respected

+ if you long to feel security, peace, and acceptance

+ if you want your life to mean something important and feel you are truly making a difference

+ if you yearn to understand why you were created and fulfill your purpose for existing

+ if you desire to experience true power and strength in your life

. . . then set yourself to knowing God in the profoundly intimate way that He created you and saved you to experience.

Follow the example of the greatest earthly ruler of Israel, King David—a man who was not only a courageous warrior and brilliant military strategist but also an accomplished musician and writer. He declared, "My soul waits in silence for God only, for my hope is from Him. He only is my rock and my salvation, my stronghold; I shall not be shaken" (Ps. 62:5–6).

King David lived a strong life, and this verse shows us why—because of his reverence, trust, confidence, dependence upon, and focus on God. David was not a perfect man by any means—far from it. But in effect he said, "God, here is my heart. I am willing to unwrap myself before You. My soul, my spirit, and everything I am belongs to You. I am holding nothing back, because You are my only hope and You make my life strong."

And because of his unyielding love for and commitment to God, the Lord did incredible things through King David—including the greatest expansion of Israel's territory in its history. But even more important, He provided the Savior of the world through David's family's line. Certainly, that's success by anyone's standards.

No one can deny that David had a personal relationship with God and true intimacy with Him. In fact, the Lord declared, "I have found David the son of Jesse, a man after My heart, who will do all My will" (Acts 13:22).

A man after God's heart—high praise, indeed. And three thousand years after David lived, we're still talking about what the Lord did through him.

Isn't that the kind of person you want to be? The person about whom God says, "That's my son/daughter—a child after My heart. And I am going to do astounding things through him/her." Because when you are a person after God's own heart, He promises, "I will instruct you and teach you in the way you should go; I will counsel you with My eye upon You" (Ps. 32:8). That, friend, is the life that endures—a strong life. An abundant life that is set on things above. And it is the only life truly worth living.

5

YOUR CONVICTIONS ABOUT PRAYER

Grocery List or Marching Orders?

Whenever I travel, I'm amazed by how many of the people I meet feel like they know me. Usually, it is because God has worked through what I've said to minister to them—and, of course, I am very grateful for that. But they feel a great deal of familiarity with me because they've listened to my sermons, read my books and articles, and heard my stories. So they do know a lot about me. And they approach me as if I were an old friend, as if I should be as acquainted with them as they are with me.

I understand that. I try to be transparent in my sermons and books, so it is natural for others to feel close to me. But the truth of the matter is that they only know some facts *about* me. They don't know *me*. They may have a good idea about my character, likes and dislikes, and even the way I operate. But that isn't the totality of who I am as a person. I have thoughts and feelings that I share only with those closest to me. Some things I don't even reveal to them—I talk about them only with God.

I mean no disrespect by saying that. I merely wish to make the point that in order to truly know a person, you have to walk with him or her through the stages and struggles of life—through the valleys of difficulty and the mountains of success. You have to hear that person's heart.

Likewise, we sometimes think we know God because we've listened to sermons, read books, and done all the good things Christians are supposed to do. But these activities alone don't help us to truly know *Him*. We've heard *about* Him, but as we talked about in the previous chapter, we do not have the profound interaction with the Lord our Savior that we were created for. So how do we do so?

If you've listened to me for any time at all, you know the answer is prayer. I cover the importance of prayer in depth in my books *Prayer: The Ultimate Conversation, Handle with Prayer,* and *How to Listen to God,* so I won't go through all of that here. But I do want to talk about how your *beliefs* about prayer affect whether or not you stand strong.

For example, you may be a person who prays a great deal. Perhaps you have a list of people you intercede for—you continually cover their illnesses, infirmities, and afflictions in your daily quiet time with the Lord. Likewise, you share your heart with the Father. You let God know everything that's bothering you. Yet something is still missing from your relationship with Him. You do not feel close to Him. You do not sense His wisdom guiding your steps or His resurrection power fueling your obedience to Him. Why?

The answer is quite simple, really. We all have friends who talk so much that we can never get a word in. Even when they ask us questions about how we are or how our family is doing, we can barely open our mouths before they are off on another train of thought. Sadly, that's how most of us are with God. We talk, talk, talk and don't stop to listen. Oh, we may ask Him about His will or to give us wisdom, but we usu-ally don't give Him much time to respond before we're giving Him our opinion of what He should do.

> *We may ask God about His will or to give us wisdom, but we usually don't give Him much time to respond.*

But if you really want to know someone, you have to listen—and that goes double for God. God's every word has meaning and impact. He does not speak merely to be heard. He speaks the very words of life that will absolutely transform you from the inside out.

WHAT IS PRAYER?

This is why prayer is an incredibly important aspect of the Christian life. How else can you get to know the Lord if you are not listening to Him? Not to what people are saying about Him, but to *God Himself.* Listening is the key to intimacy and to walking in a manner pleasing to Him.

So what exactly is prayer? *Prayer is an intimate dialogue with the Lord for the purposes of learning from Him and about Him, seeking His wisdom and provision, understanding His will, fellowshipping with Him, and worshipping Him.* Prayer is an openhearted inter-change with the One who cares about you most. It truly is the ultimate conversation—your opportunity to seek understanding from your Creator, your chance to ask the Lord of all that exists to deliver you in the areas where you cannot help yourself, and your privilege to know Him better.

This is why prayer is the root of your personal relationship with God. Its purpose is to strengthen and deepen your intimacy with Him. And it is why I so often say, "Listening to God is essential to walking with God." You cannot get to know Him if you do all the speaking.

Of course, we do so much of the talking because of the ease of reception. We can hear ourselves. Ever notice how long you will sit in front of the radio, television, or computer without saying anything? Why? Because you are receiving what another person is transmitting. If you talked back, he or she would not hear you. In a sense, when we pray, we are like those broadcasters. We speak as if the One listening to us cannot or will not respond.

True, it is not easy to hear God. It takes focus, concentration, and even training, because His manner of communicating with us is different from what we're accustomed to. It is much easier to fill the silences with our own voices, so we talk about our needs and the afflictions of others. Of course, as we learned in the previous chapter, this is a crucial part of intimacy. We must be transparent, honest, and open to God in every area of life. Unfortunately, this is where some people stop the conversation.

But listening to God is an equally important part of the process—even if it is a more difficult one. We must have a patient focus on Him, eagerly watching for what He is doing and saying in our lives. After all, He is God! You have the incredible privilege of walking with the Lord of all Creation, so you should not take that for granted. Ecclesiastes 5:1–2 reminds us:

Guard your steps as you go to the house of God and draw near to listen rather than to offer the sacrifice of fools; for they do not know they are doing evil. Do not be hasty in word or impulsive in thought to bring up a matter in the presence of God. For God is in heaven and you are on the earth; therefore let your words be few.

This verse touches on the important fact that your attitude about the Lord influences your interactions with Him—whether or not you are respecting Him as the Ruler and Owner of all creation.

We're motivated to be near those we value highly. We want to learn from them and express our appreciation. We recognize that the opportunities to be around them are a gift. The same is true in our relationships with God.

However, if you have a faulty and dejected view of the Lord— thinking He is not actively engaged in your life or that He is in some way cruel—you won't want to interact with Him. None of us wants to spend time with someone who is indifferent or mean.

On the other hand, if you respect Him as God Almighty— realizing the awesome privilege you have of being in His presence and enjoying His love—then you'll be overjoyed to spend time with Him and look with anticipation to what He has to say.

Likewise, your view of the Lord will affect the *content* of your prayers—what you say to Him. What you communicate during your time alone with the Father will reveal an enormous amount about what you really think of Him. It will also explain your enthusiasm or reluctance to enter into His presence.

Are you going before the Lord to learn more about Him,

discover His awesome plans for your life, and worship Him? Or do you list all your desires and the things you would like Him to do?

Are you seeking His will because you know His purposes for you are better than anything you could possibly imagine on your own? Or do you bring Him your plans, hoping He'll bless them? Is your prayer time self-centered or God-centered?

If you're consistently fixated on yourself as you fellowship with the Father, then your focus is misplaced.

If you're consistently fixated on yourself as you fellowship with the Father, then your focus is misplaced. You are missing out on one of the greatest blessings you can have as a believer—the joy of being enveloped by His awesome presence.

So examine what you truly believe about God and prayer, especially if you have trouble drawing close to Him or experiencing His presence.

TALKING TO GOD

With this in mind, let's think about how we talk to the Lord. As we just saw in Ecclesiastes 5:1–2, it is incredibly important to approach God with reverence. So even when we express ourselves to Him, we need to remember that the focus is not on us but on His incredible character, love, goodness, wisdom, and ability.

Throughout the years, I've heard people teach an easy acronym that helps us remember to put God first and address Him in a manner worthy of His divinity as we pray: ACTS, which stands for *adoration, confession, thanksgiving,* and *supplication.*

Now, my personal conviction is that prayer is an intimate conversation, and most intimate conversations do not involve an outline. They flow naturally out of our love relationship with the other person. However, if you are new to a truly intimate conversation with God, ACTS will help train you to maintain a right attitude when you talk to your loving heavenly Father.

Adoration. Our conversations with the Lord should always begin with a reminder of who He is. And of course, when we really think about the awesomeness of God, we are led into deep and meaningful worship. So as you communicate with the Father, praise Him for His goodness to you and His wonderful attributes.

Confession. Our interaction with the Lord should also involve a desire to rid ourselves of anything that hinders our relationship with Him. So whenever you approach His throne of grace, ask God if there is anything in you that is displeasing to Him. As He reveals issues in your life to deal with, agree with Him, ask Him how He would like you to change, and commit to walk in His ways.

Thanksgiving. As God reveals Himself to you and you realize all the amazing ways He is working in your life, give Him thanks. He is supplying your needs and leading you in holiness and wisdom in ways that you could never have imagined. So express your gratefulness for His presence, provision, and protection.

Supplication. Finally, talk to God openly and honestly about what is going on in your life.

+ *First, talk to Him about Kingdom business:* the needs and difficulties at your church, for the missionaries you know, for the persecuted church—your brothers and sisters in the faith who are suffering for the sake of the gospel, and for those who have experienced tragedy and/or natural disasters. Ask the Father if there is any way you can alleviate the burdens of your brothers and sisters in Christ or reach someone who is hurting with the Good News of salvation.

+ *Next, pray for the needs of others*: for those in your life who are sick, are facing financial difficulties, or are struggling in their relationships. Again, ask the Lord for wisdom about how you can help those close to you.

+ *Finally, pray for your own needs, remembering to seek God's will about what you should do.* I have found that once I praise the Father, confess my sins, and give Him thanks, my problems and needs don't appear so overwhelming or impossible. I believe that you will discover the same thing—that once you experience the greatness and love of God, you will be filled with confidence about everything you face.

LISTENING TO GOD

As you may have noticed, listening to God is already part of the process of prayer even when you are talking to Him. When you ask the Father if there is anything in you that is displeasing to Him, you must actively listen to Him in order to confess and repent. When you seek the Lord's wisdom about the difficulties you face or how to help others, you must set yourself to hear His response. If you truly want His answers to your requests, you need to pay attention to His direction.

Likewise, if you want intimacy with God, to know His will for your life, and to stand strong when the winds of trial assail you, you will need to heed what He is saying. This is why prayer is an essential part of His communication with us that affects our walk with Him. We're receiving our marching orders—the guidance to finding what we were created to accomplish.

This is where the real difference comes for our lives. When we stop short of listening to God, the Christian life will remain uninspired, unremarkable, and weak. Because when we don't listen, we are continuing in our own wisdom.

But when we *do* listen to God, walking in His will, He will direct us in ways we would never conceive. And when we believe and obey Him, He takes us places and does things through us that defy imagination. Likewise, He sustains us through situations that would normally defeat even the strongest person.

> *When we stop short of listening to God, the Christian life will remain uninspired, unremarkable, and weak.*

For example, consider the problem King Jehoshaphat and the people of Judah experienced when they were attacked by three armies on the same day—the forces of the Moabites, Ammonites, and Meunites (2 Chr. 20:1–30). Even one of these invaders would have been too much for the weak nation of Judah—defending against this threefold assault was impossible. Perhaps you've experienced such confusing circumstances. You just don't know how to proceed because there are so many factors to consider. You have no way of figuring out how all the pieces work together or how you could ever overcome them. What can you do?

Second Chronicles 20 tells us:

Judah gathered together to seek help from the Lord ...
Then Jehoshaphat stood in the assembly of Judah and Jerusalem, in the house of the Lord before the new court, and
he said, "O Lord, the God of our fathers, are You not God
in the heavens? And are You not ruler over all the king-
doms of the nations? Power and might are in Your hand
so that no one can stand against You. Did You not, O our
God, drive out the inhabitants of this land before Your people Israel and give it to the descendants of Abraham Your
friend forever? ... Now behold, the sons of Ammon and
Moab and Mount Seir ... are rewarding us by coming to
drive us out from Your possession which You have given us
as an inheritance. O our God, will You not judge them? For
we are powerless before this great multitude who are coming against us; nor do we know what to do, but our eyes are
on You." (vv. 4–7, 10–12)

We are powerless ... nor do we know what to do. How often
have you felt that very prayer in your own heart? *This issue is too
great and I just don't know how to navigate the perplexing nature of
the circumstances I find myself in. I see only defeat in my future.*

Sadly, what we often do in prayer is lay out our plans before
God and expect Him to bless them; or after we pray, we make our
own battle plans and move forward. We stop short of listening.
But that is not what King Jehoshaphat and the people of Judah
did. They understood that God sees the situation from a perspective of profound clarity and wisdom. Again, 2 Chronicles 20
reports:

The Spirit of the Lord came upon Jahaziel . . . and he said, "Listen, all Judah and the inhabitants of Jerusalem and King Jehoshaphat: thus says the Lord to you, 'Do not fear or be dismayed because of this great multitude, for the battle is not yours but God's. Tomorrow go down against them. Behold, they will come up by the ascent of Ziz, and you will find them at the end of the valley in front of the wilderness of Jeruel. You need not fight in this battle; station yourselves, stand and see the salvation of the Lord on your behalf, O Judah and Jerusalem.' Do not fear or be dismayed; tomorrow go out to face them, for the Lord is with you." (vv. 14–17)

Who would fight the battle? The Lord would. The next day, instead of taking up arms, they employed the unprecedented military strategy of taking up their instruments and praising God with them. And what happened next was nothing short of miraculous.

When they began singing and praising, the Lord set ambushes against the sons of Ammon, Moab, and Mount Seir, who had come against Judah; so they were routed. For the sons of Ammon and Moab rose up against the inhabitants of Mount Seir destroying them completely; and when they had finished with the inhabitants of Seir, they helped to destroy one another. (2 Chr. 20:22–23)

God, in His wisdom, understood the enemies' plans, faults, and blind spots—and used these to set them against each other and gain the victory for Judah. If the Judahites had fought the battle with their own strength and wisdom, they would have failed. But because they listened to the Lord, they saw His supernatural work. God turned an impossible situation into an overwhelming triumph for His people and an undeniable warning to the surrounding nations.

The same is true for you, and it is why I always say that when you fight your battles on your knees, you win every time. Friend, do you realize *why* the troubles you face are so complicated and confounding—far beyond your ability to reason them out? It is because the Lord your God *wants you* to rely on *His* wisdom and strength—to know you have access to the omniscient mind and omnipotent power of the One who loves you and saves you. This is why James 1:5 promises, "If any of you lacks wisdom, let him ask of God, who gives to all generously and without reproach, and it will be given to him." Because an intimate relationship with God, where we rely upon Him rather than our own strength or insight, is how we stand strong. The key is *listening* to Him.

> *Do you realize why the troubles you face are far beyond your ability to reason them out? It is because the Lord your God wants you to rely on His wisdom and strength.*

STILL SPEAKING

Of course, doubt may still trouble your heart: *Does God speak to us today as He did then? And if He does, how can I be sure I hear Him?* Absolutely He does! The Lord most certainly continues in communication with His people. He never wants us to approach Him with a "hope so" attitude: "I hope He hears me. I hope He will speak to me." Rather, the Father wants us to *know* that He is both listening and expressing Himself to us.

Think about it: *God wants us to do His will.* In order for us to carry out the Lord's plan for our lives, we have to know what He has called us to be and do. It would be out of character for the Father to hide His will and then expect us to walk in it. In fact, I've often seen that, if necessary, He will move heaven and earth to show us His will.

So we should be confident that our good, loving, and powerful heavenly Father is always available to communicate with us. His response to us may not be what we expect, but He never fails to reply if we're willing to listen.

Therefore, the real question is not "Does God still speak today?" but "Am I listening as He speaks to me?"

The Lord unquestionably has a plan for each of our lives. We saw this when we discussed Ephesians 2:10: "We are His workmanship, created in Christ Jesus for good works, which God prepared beforehand so that we would walk in them." But what is especially essential for us to understand is that He is *continually* instructing us about His purposes—patiently revealing Himself and His will to us through every detail of our experience. The Father communicates with us through each situation we encounter, but hearing Him is dependent upon our anticipating and paying attention to His instruction.

So our challenge is to *expect* Him to reveal Himself and intentionally *apply* what He says. To do so, we must have an open and willing heart—regardless of what we are facing—and await His leadership with hope and faith. We must persistently be of this mind-set: "The Lord has something to say to me, and I'm not going to miss it!"

So how do we do this? The key, friend, is in changing the *way* we listen.

A NEW WAY OF HEARING

Most of us are *passive* listeners. We will sit and listen to a sermon or a teaching session, but almost immediately afterward we forget what was said. We don't listen with the intention of relating what is said to our lives, or examining our hearts.

In other words, we *listen* but we do not *hear*. What has been communicated does not make an impact. For example, suppose that I asked you:

+ What did your pastor preach this past Sunday?

+ What Scripture passage did he talk about?

+ How are you actively applying the message to your life?

Most people could not answer those questions without looking at their notes. Perhaps you couldn't either. This is because we are not conditioned to do so. We may know how to sit through a service politely, but often our thoughts are far from what is actually being preached.

But that isn't how you hear God. Rather, in everything, you must be actively asking, "Lord, what are You saying to me? How should this influence my life so I can better conform to Your image and be more faithful to You?"

In other words, we must become *purposeful* listeners. James 1:22–25 instructs:

> Prove yourselves doers of the word, and not merely hearers who delude themselves. For if anyone is a hearer of the word and not a doer, he is like a man who looks at his natural face in a mirror; for once he has looked at himself and gone away, he has immediately forgotten what kind of person he was. But one who looks intently at the perfect law, the law of liberty, and abides by it, not having become a forgetful hearer but an effectual doer, this man will be blessed in what he does.

We must listen intently with the purpose of learning, understanding, and applying the truth to our lives. We must anticipate God's direction and heed His instruction. The Father has something important to say to us that will impact us not only today but will also impact *eternity*.

Just think about all the reasons *why* God speaks to us.

First, the Father speaks to build our intimate relationship with Him. This, of course, has implications forever. We see this in Jesus' earthly life—He was constantly in prayer because of the immense importance of having this vital connection with the Father (Mark 1:35). In fact, John 17:3 tells us, "This is eternal life, that they may know You, the only true God, and Jesus Christ whom You have sent." The very nature of our everlasting life is based on, fulfilled in, and characterized by our relationship with God. And I believe we will spend forever finding out just what that means.

Second, God speaks to communicate His will to us and empower us to carry it out. After His resurrection, Jesus gave the disciples the incredible assignment of reaching the whole world with the gospel (Matt. 28:18–20). Do you think those fishermen knew what to do? Of course they didn't. They needed God's wisdom on how to proceed. So they prayed (Acts 1:14). And when other activities began to fill their time, they restated their purpose: "We will devote ourselves to prayer and to the ministry of the word" (Acts 6:4). We see that the apostles regarded this as the most important business of their lives so they could know how to carry out Christ's commission. We must also recognize that all of God's most effective servants have been mighty in prayer. Their gifts and backgrounds may have been different, but they were all committed to listening to the Father so He could guide and empower them for the tasks they carried out.

Next, God speaks to grow and mature us spiritually. As we fellowship with the Lord, He helps us to see our circumstances from His point of view. He helps us get the most out of every challenge— stretching our faith, pointing out our blind spots, teaching us His ways, and helping us to rely upon Him. He also conforms us to His character (Rom. 8:29, 12:2) and produces the fruit of the Spirit through us: love, joy, peace, patience, kindness, goodness, faithfulness, gentleness, and self-control (Gal. 5:22–23).

Additionally, God speaks to liberate us from sin, bondage, and fear. Through prayer, the Father convicts us of sin and teaches us how to be free of it. He also reveals the painful wounds in our lives and heals us of our bondage—areas that are usually rooted in and produce fear. By setting us free of our sins and wounds, God is also liberating us so we can become all He created us to be without those encumbrances.

God also speaks to fill us with His peace. Philippians 4:6–7 instructs, "Be anxious for nothing, but in everything by prayer and supplication with thanksgiving let your requests be made known to God. And the peace of God, which surpasses all comprehension, will guard your hearts and your minds in Christ Jesus." Why does His peace garrison us about when we pray? Because we are reminded of who it is that fights for us—the Lord Almighty Himself.

> *As we fellowship with the Lord, He helps us to see our circumstances from His point of view.*

Finally, God speaks to protect us from the enemy. As believers, we face a very real adversary and spiritual warfare that can affect us in untold ways. Ephesians 6:12 confirms: "Our struggle is not against flesh and blood, but against the rulers, against the powers, against the world forces of this darkness, against the spiritual forces of wickedness in the heavenly places." But to do battle in a spiritual war, you have to fight with spiritual weapons. Through prayer, God prepares us to resist the devil, sin, and temptation. How? First, He helps us avoid the traps and pitfalls that the enemy sets for us. Second, He helps us identify the triggers the enemy uses to entice us to sin and uproots them. Third, because the enemy influences us on the spiritual level when we pray, God builds up our spiritual strength and defenses. For example, the Lord may defend us by sending Scripture to mind when a temptation arises. In other words, He teaches us to use the spiritual arsenal He has already given us.

The point is, when God speaks, it is important and beneficial to you—eternally so! Would you want to miss what He is saying in any of those areas? Of course not.

THE ATTITUDE OF TRIUMPH

Now, I have often spoken about how God speaks to us—through His Word, the Holy Spirit, circumstances, other people, and prayer. In fact, in chapter 2 we discussed in depth why it is so important to pay close attention to Scripture in order to learn from the Father. The important role of prayer is that it connects the other four components—the Bible, the Holy Spirit, circumstances, and other people—in a supernatural way that God uses to communicate with us. Through our time in communion with Him, the Father takes what we are learning in Scripture, the situations we are encountering in our lives, and what we are gathering from others and through the promptings of the Holy Spirit convicts our hearts—showing us how they relate to one another and how He is influencing us through them.

This is why 1 Thessalonians 5:17 tells us, "Pray without ceasing." That does not signify we are to be continually on our knees in intercession without regard to anything else. Rather, it means that we should become accustomed to taking everything we hear, see, read, and experience to God and asking Him what we should do with it. We should consistently ask Him, "Father, are You saying something to me through the circumstances I am facing? How do You want me to apply what I've read, seen, and heard to my life? Are You working in some way that You want me to notice?"

This is how we become purposeful listeners—always seeking, attentive, expectant, and obedient. So to have the triumphant attitude of a purposeful listener:

Pray regularly, in private. Set aside time to be alone with God. Find a quiet place and devote yourself to the One who has the greatest ability to help you.

As you pray, do not ignore anything God brings to mind. The seemingly random thoughts that arise when you're praying may be something the Lord is trying to deal with in your own life.

Have God's Word open in front of you and reflect on it. Meditate on the biblical passages the Lord leads you to. Read them over thoughtfully and ask God to help you understand what He is saying to you and how to apply it to your life.

Ask God for verification. What you believe you are hearing through the Holy Spirit, circumstances, people, and in prayer *must always be consistent with Scripture.* Nothing the Lord tells you will ever contradict His Word, so always ask God to confirm His message to you through the Bible.

Approach the Lord with obedience as your goal. Set your heart to submit to whatever God calls you to do (James 1:22). Before He responds to your requests, the Father may want you to deal with sin in your life. Until you repent and surrender to Him, that sin will keep you from experiencing His best and enjoying a close relationship with Him. Submit yourself to His wisdom. Likewise, the Lord may call you to take steps of obedience that you just don't understand. Obey Him anyway. Trust that He has good reasons for everything He asks you to do even when you cannot yet see them.

At times, pray with others. The Holy Spirit will speak to you through the prayers of other believers, and the Lord will work through that time together to bring unity to a group. It is difficult to harbor resentment and unforgiveness for someone when you are regularly baring your souls to the Father in one accord.

Seek God expectantly. The Lord promises to speak to you, so anticipate that He will even if for a time you hear nothing but silence.

Wait patiently before God. Sometimes it will take time for the Lord to respond to your requests. You may never know why it is that God is delaying His answers to the cries of your heart—it may be because He is engineering your circumstances or teaching you to trust in Him despite your situation. The point is, *keep praying* because God *will* answer you. We see this in a wonderfully vivid way in Daniel 10. Daniel had seen a vision from the Lord but did not understand it. In fact, in verse 2, Daniel said he "had been mourning" because of it. So for three weeks he prayed without ceasing.

Perhaps you understand the depth of his despair. The Lord allows trials to assail your life, but there is no explanation, so sorrow fills your heart. Yet after three weeks, a messenger from God revealed to him: "Do not be afraid, Daniel, for from the first day that you set your heart on understanding this and on humbling yourself before your God, *your words were heard*, and I have come in response to your words. But the prince of the kingdom of Persia was withstanding me for twenty-one days" (vv. 12–13; emphasis added).

Likewise, there may be forces standing in the way of God's will for you that you could not possibly imagine. Wait patiently for the Father, because He will certainly answer you and triumph on your behalf.

Finally, be diligent and do not give up. Jesus taught the disciples "a parable to show that at all times they ought to pray and not to lose heart" (Luke 18:1). In it, a widow, without other recourse, repeatedly asks a judge for protection from an opponent until he relents. Jesus tells His disciples, "Even he rendered a just decision in the end. So don't you think God will surely give justice to His chosen people who cry out to him day and night? Will He keep putting them off?" (v. 7 NLT).

You may find yourself in a position like that widow's—with no resources to rely upon except God's provision and protection. The opportunity for discouragement

"From the first day that you set your heart on understanding this and on humbling yourself before your God, your words were heard."

exists because you do not see the Lord at work and you may feel as if He does not hear you. But be assured, friend, *He does.* You need to keep clinging to and seeking the Father. He is merely working in the unseen. Stay in close fellowship with Him so your strength will not fail and you will not lose heart (Luke 22:32).

AN INCREASINGLY STRONG FOUNDATION

Friend, if you want a strong foundation, you must have an intimate relationship with God. And if you want this kind of close fellowship with the Father, the way is through communicating with Him in prayer. This is why I have included prayer in the foundation section of this book.

As we noted in the first chapter, Jesus said, "Everyone who hears these words of Mine and acts on them, may be compared to a wise man who built his house on the rock. And the rain fell, and the floods came, and the winds blew and slammed against that house; and yet it did not fall, for it had been founded on the rock" (Matt. 7:24–25). How can we know Christ's words without being in Scripture? We can't. Likewise, how can we act on His words if we aren't in active, intimate communion with Him? Again, we can't. Without hearing from God, we can go only as far as our understanding of Scripture takes us, and that is simply not deep enough to provide the foundation we need.

In the subsequent chapters, we will be talking about what we build our lives *with*. But it is of utmost importance that you make prayer and that intimate relationship with God your first priority. Because everything else in your life rests on it. The stronger your relationship with the Father, the more powerful and resilient your life. The more profound your relationship with Him, the tougher and more unshakable your foundation.

We can see this so clearly in the lives of the disciples. I mentioned earlier that after Jesus rose from the dead and ascended to heaven, the disciples devoted themselves to prayer. We often talk about the fact that Jesus told them to wait for the empowering of the Holy Spirit. But we do not often talk about *how* they waited. Acts 1:12–14 reports:

> They returned to Jerusalem from the mount called Olivet, which is near Jerusalem, a Sabbath day's journey away. When they had entered the city, they went up to the upper room where they were staying; that is, Peter and John and

James and Andrew, Philip and Thomas, Bartholomew and Matthew, James the son of Alphaeus, and Simon the Zealot, and Judas the son of James. *These all with one mind were continually devoting themselves to prayer* (emphasis added).

In that time, they were listening to God, strengthening their relationship with Him, preparing for what was ahead, fighting the spiritual battles, and getting their marching orders from Him.

It was only after this time of devoted prayer that the Holy Spirit fell upon them.

God had to prepare them before He could empower them. The Lord had to take the frightened disciples who ran away from Christ's Crucifixion (Matt. 26:56)—and even denied knowing Jesus (John 18:15–27)—and make them into men with such unshakable faith that they rejoiced "that they had been considered worthy to suffer shame for His name" (Acts 5:41). And He did it to a great extent through that incredible, transformative time in prayer.

If prayer was that important to Jesus and to the disciples, it should be imperative to us as well. Because without a doubt purposeful, obedient, believing prayer is key to standing strong and seeing God fulfill His great and eternal plans through us.

Part 2

BUILT WITH

*If any man builds on the foundation with gold, silver,
precious stones, wood, hay, straw,
each man's work will become evident;
for the day will show it because it is to be revealed with fire,
and the fire itself will test the quality of each man's work.*
—1 Corinthians 3:12–13

6

YOUR CONVICTIONS ABOUT YOUR LIFE

Ownership or Stewardship?

Second Chronicles 3:17 tells us that when Solomon had the Temple constructed, "He erected the pillars in front of the temple . . . and named the one on the right Jachin and the one on the left Boaz." This was so that those who gazed upon that grand and beautiful structure—a structure that represented the presence of the Lord among His people—would always remember two important things.

First, the name of the right or northern pillar, *Jachin*, means "He establishes." It is God who begins and builds anything of importance in this world and in eternity.

And second, the name of the left or southern pillar was *Boaz*, which signifies "by Him is he mighty." It was by this pillar that a king would stand to instruct the people and give his decrees, demonstrating that his strength, authority, and success were given to him by the Lord alone.

What a beautiful testimony to us as we continue to talk about standing strong. After all, our foundation is God Himself. But as we said in the first chapter, it's not just what you build *on* that counts, but also *how* you build and what you build *with*. After all, when you have an intimate relationship with the Lord, something good will naturally be produced by it. Something strong will be constructed on that foundation.

In fact, interacting with God in prayer is inevitably *life changing*, because He always calls us to His higher ways, challenging us to pursue His goals and to be more like Him. This experience will always be beyond what we know and understand and will always stretch us—because He is growing us spiritually and conforming us to His own image (Rom. 8:29).

I have found that this inevitable "stretching" is one of the reasons some people don't want to pray. The Lord confronts things in their lives that they don't want to let go of. Or He calls them to missions that are too great or challenging, and they become fearful.

But the Lord is God, and 1 Corinthians 6:19–20 tells us: "Do you not know that your body is a temple of the Holy Spirit who is in you, whom you have from God, and that you are not your own? For you have been bought with a price: therefore glorify God in your body." We have to make a decision about whom we belong to and who has the wiser, more powerful plans for our lives. Like the Temple in Jerusalem, if we are going to stand strong, our lives must be built with the pillars of *Jachin* and *Boaz*—or, as I like to call them, *trust* and *obedience*.

First, we must understand that it is God who establishes (*Jachin*). He is the One who forms us, makes the plans for our lives, and He is the One we must *trust* with every step on our path. But also, we must realize that it is by His wisdom and power that we are mighty (*Boaz*). And so we can *obey* the Lord no matter what He calls us to do, with confidence that He will enable us to complete whatever assignment He gives us.

THE NECESSITY OF PLANTING FAITH

Faith, of course, is the requirement for serving God that we find in Hebrews 11:6: "Without faith it is impossible to please Him, for he who comes to God must believe that He is and that He is a rewarder of those who seek Him." Without faith—without the kind of trust that results in obedience—it is not possible to honor the Lord as God. Faith in what?

First, according to the verse we just read, the person who approaches the Lord *"must believe that He is"*—that He exists. We believe in God's existence with our minds, but do we believe it in a practical way? Do we demonstrate with our lives that the Lord is indeed the God of all creation, who rules over the heavens and the earth? If He asks us to give up everything today, do we indeed trust that He will provide what we need tomorrow? And do we have enough respect for Him to do as He asks?

Second, the person who seeks the Father must believe that *"He is a rewarder of those who seek Him."* In other words, do we trust God's character—that He does indeed desire good for us? That He works for our benefit? When everything is going well, it's not difficult to confess that He, indeed, works to bless us. But when our situation falls apart, we are tempted to doubt that everything will work together for our benefit and according to His good plan—eventually.

Whether or not you believe that God exists and is a rewarder of those who seek Him will shape the character of your life. You see, there are consequences for our actions and what we believe. For every decision we make, there is a result. That does not mean all consequences are bad—some are wonderful. The point is that our lives are shaped by the truth we find in Galatians 6:7: "Whatever a man sows, this he will also reap." We may not see it right away, but our choices shape our lives and even what we become in eternity. I like to think of it like this: *You reap what you sow, more than you sow, and later than you sow.*

Do we trust God's character—that He does indeed desire good for us? That He works for our benefit?

Consider a farmer. *He reaps what he sows.* If he wants to grow tomatoes, he is a fool to plant apple seeds.

He reaps more than he sows. The farmer knows that if he plants a small seed, a large plant can grow from it. In other words, the little things that are rooted will become much bigger.

And he reaps later than he sows. No farmer goes out the next day after planting seeds looking for a huge harvest. That would be silly. He knows that it takes a long time for things to mature fully.

This is true for us spiritually as well. Every day that we live, we have decisions we must make. And every choice comes back to what we just looked at in Hebrews 11:6: *Do we believe that God exists? And do we have confidence that He is a rewarder of those who seek Him?* Do we really trust God's character—that He is working—all things for our good? Our choices to believe or not believe are the seeds that are planted in our lives, and with each decision, we are either nurturing our relationship with God or destroying it.

We are reaping *what* we sow. We are either growing in our intimacy with the Father or in rebellion against Him.

We are reaping *more than* we sow. Our decisions to believe God or not believe affect far more than we could ever imagine. Consider Adam and Eve. Perhaps they thought, "It is just a piece of fruit. How much harm could it really do?" But that act of disobedience has affected humanity for eternity. Likewise, our choices may not seem important, but they impact our families, our communities, and even the generations after us.

Finally, we are reaping *later than* we sow. We do not know how the choices God gives us are building us for tomorrow, but we do know they are working toward an important harvest. Philippians 1:6 tells us, "He who began a good work in you will perfect it until the day of Christ Jesus." Consider what that really means. It indicates that when you do something with trust in and obedience to God, it will continue to have increasing ramifications and blessings in eternity.

A KEY TO DECISION MAKING: *REAPING WHAT WE SOW*

Understanding that what we plant has lasting consequences is a key to our decision-making process. We realize that in order to be wise, we must always look beyond our immediate choices to the consequences that will follow. Many people fail to consider the long-term effects of how they live. But as followers of Jesus, we know that every action has an impact for good or evil in an eternal sense. Our choices determine the quality and influence not only of our lives but can also affect the lives of those around us and who come after us forever.

The classic example of this is Abraham. We know that at the age of seventy-five, God promised to make him the father of a great nation (Gen. 12:1–4). However, after about ten years of waiting for the Lord to provide them with a child, he and Sarah grew weary. I'm sure that the burden of their enduring childlessness had to weigh on them greatly. Day after day, they must have wondered what was wrong: Why wasn't God providing for them? Eventually, it appears that Sarah came to the conclusion that she was the one hindering the promise from coming to fruition. So she came up with a plan utilizing a strategy that was a common practice in their culture. Abraham would conceive a child with her Egyptian servant Hagar. What could possibly go wrong?

In order to be wise, we must always look beyond our immediate choices to the consequences that will follow.

Of course, we know that a great deal of trouble resulted from that decision. A baby named Ishmael was born, and his offspring eventually became some of the Arab nations (Gen. 25:18) that have been a source of tremendous conflict for Abraham's rightful heir, Isaac, and his descendants, the people of Israel. In other words, Abraham's disobedience is still impacting the world today with all the conflict in the Middle East. His actions are bearing consequences for his people more than *four thousand* years after he lived. He certainly reaped a lot more than he sowed.

The point is that in the choices we make, our instinct is to follow the world or our own wisdom, which is disobedience. But we are not going to like the result. As we saw earlier from Proverbs 14:12 and 16:25, "There is a way which seems right to a man, but its end is the way of death." What we reap from disobedience is sin, strife, corruption, and destruction.

But when we follow God, agree with His ways, and obey Him, we will reap amazing blessings:

+ Intimacy with Him—our Creator and the Lord of the universe, with all the rights and privileges of a relationship with Him

+ A productive life full of purpose and significance

+ The fruit of the Spirit—love, joy, peace, patience, kindness, goodness, faithfulness, gentleness, and self-control

+ A lasting, positive impact on those around us

+ Eternal assurance and rewards

I happen to believe the choice is clear because obedience to God always brings blessings.

RAMIFICATIONS BEYOND ESTIMATION: REAPING MORE THAN WE SOW

Friend, do not ever underestimate how important your obedience to God is for your life here and in eternity. The book of Esther gives us an amazing illustration of this.

If you recall, Esther was a Jewish girl chosen from all the virgins of the land to be the queen of the ruler of Persia and Media, King Ahasuerus (some Bible translations use the name Xerxes). During that time, a wicked man named Haman the Agagite arose, and his goal was to exterminate the Jews. The basic point of the book of Esther is to show how God worked through Esther and her uncle Mordecai to save the Jewish people.

But do you realize that Haman should never have existed in the first place?

Hundreds of years earlier, God instructed King Saul of Israel to go to war against the Amalekites. Through the prophet Samuel, the Lord said, "I will punish Amalek for what he did to Israel . . . Go and strike Amalek and utterly destroy all that he has, and do not spare him; but put to death both man and woman, child and infant, ox and sheep, camel and donkey" (1 Sam. 15:2–3).

Although Saul did go to battle against the Amalekites and even defeated them, he failed to obey all of God's command. First Samuel 15:9 tells us, "Saul and the people *spared Agag* and the best of the sheep, the oxen, the fatlings, the lambs, and all that was good, and *were not willing to destroy them utterly*" (emphasis added). In other words, they disobeyed God *and allowed King Agag to live* because they believed they knew better.

What could it matter, right? After all, the Lord's command seemed harsh and unreasonable. What harm could it do for Saul to spare King Agag and some of the wonderful livestock he owned?

Yet generations later, the Lord's wisdom shone through. Because, of course, Haman the Agagite was a descendant of the king Saul was supposed to have killed—King Agag.

Consider the ramifications. If Haman had succeeded in destroying the Jews, he would have cut off the family line of the promised Messiah. There would have been no Jesus, which would mean no salvation for any of us. So Saul's seemingly insignificant act of disobedience would have had eternally detrimental consequences for *all* of humanity.

But here is where the story grows even more interesting.

You see, Esther and her family were descended from a man named Shimei. And when you look back in the Old Testament, you find an intriguing story about him. You see, Shimei didn't like King David at all and was outright belligerent to him. Second Samuel 16:7–8 reports, "He threw stones at David and at all the servants of King David . . . Thus Shimei said when he cursed, 'Get out, get out, you man of bloodshed, and worthless fellow!'" Imagine cursing and throwing rocks at the king of Israel! That was an act of treason worthy of death. So one of David's men said, "Why should this dead dog curse my lord the king? Let me go over now and cut off his head" (2 Sam. 16:9).

However, because of the incredible respect David had for the Lord, he decided to have mercy on Shimei. David said, "If he curses, and if the Lord has told him, 'Curse David,' then who shall say, 'Why have you done so?' . . . Let him alone and let him curse, for the Lord has told him. Perhaps the Lord will look on my affliction and return good to me instead of his cursing this day" (2 Sam. 16:10–12).

Because of David's wisdom and submission to God's will, Shimei lived, and eventually his descendants Mordecai and Esther arose to save the people of Israel from the schemes of the evil Haman.

In other words, because of Saul's *disobedience*, there was a dire existential threat to the Jews. But because of David's *obedience* to the Lord, there was someone to deliver them. These seemingly insignificant decisions not only meant life and death for the entire Jewish race but also had implications for the existence of our Savior, Jesus, and our everlasting relationship with the Father.

This is why we should never underestimate how important our obedience to God is. First John 2:17 assures us, "The world is passing away, and also its lusts; but the one who does the will of God lives forever." We do not know what all our faithfulness to Him will mean in eternity, but we do know it is far greater than we can possibly imagine. Because we reap what we sow, more than we sow, and later than we sow.

BELIEVING RATHER THAN SEEING: REAPING LATER THAN WE SOW

The principles of reaping what we sow and reaping more than we sow seem clear. As believers, we understand these concepts and live them out as best we can. But what do we do when life becomes confusing?

When God gives us a goal but does not tell us how to get there?

When what the Father asks us to do appears totally unreasonable?

When all we can see is the bad that will happen to us if we submit to Him—the persecution, the cost to ourselves and our families, the problems that will arise if we step out in faith?

When a hurricane of trouble is bearing down on us because we've obeyed the Lord, and it may seem that He has abandoned us while we are serving Him?

This is where we can truly become confused and lose hope.

Think about the disciples. In Acts 5:12–29, we're told that their ministry was very fruitful. "All the people had high regard for them. Yet more and more people believed and were brought to the Lord—crowds of both men and women" (vv. 13–14 NLT). Multitudes of people were coming to

What do we do when God gives us a goal but does not tell us how to get there?

know Jesus as their Savior. Miracles were happening on the streets of Jerusalem, and the Lord was being glorified among His people.

One would think that those who claimed to serve God would have rejoiced in such an outpouring of His power into people's lives. Sadly, "The high priest and his officials, who were Sadducees, were filled with jealousy. They arrested the apostles and put them in the public jail" (vv. 17–18). Likewise, they demanded that the disciples cease from preaching.

One might imagine the discouragement the disciples faced at that point. It is a question we are bound to ask in our hearts: *Lord, we're serving You faithfully. Why has this trouble come upon us?*

Then Acts 5:19–20 tells us, "During the night an angel of the Lord opened the gates of the prison, and taking them out he said, 'Go, stand and speak to the people in the temple the whole message of this Life.'"

Read that again. Really think about how difficult this command would have been to them. Consider the consequences the disciples faced. Certainly, it meant an even harsher punishment from the high priest and his officials if they were taken into custody again—possible beatings, further imprisonment, and even a death sentence. Most people don't witness to others, because they are afraid of being disliked, appearing ignorant, or messing up. The

Lord was asking the disciples—and us—to make a choice. Which is more important: this life or eternity?

Thankfully, Acts 5:21 testifies, "Upon hearing this, they entered into the temple about daybreak and began to teach." They went right back into the thick of battle and proclaimed the gospel. They understood that the consequences for disobeying the Lord were far greater than for disobeying the high priest. And with their lives they showed that they believed God exists and is truly a rewarder of those who seek Him. Acts 5:27–32 reports:

> When [the temple guard] had brought them, they stood them before the Council. The high priest questioned them, saying, "We gave you strict orders not to continue teaching in this name, and yet, you have filled Jerusalem with your teaching and intend to bring this man's blood upon us." But Peter and the apostles answered, "We must obey God rather than men. The God of our fathers raised up Jesus, whom you had put to death by hanging Him on a cross. He is the one whom God exalted to His right hand as a Prince and a Savior, to grant repentance to Israel, and forgiveness of sins. And we are witnesses of these things; and so is the Holy Spirit, whom God has given to those who obey Him."

Did you notice that Peter said, "We must obey God rather than men"? In other words, we obey God and leave the consequences to Him. Why? Because although the authorities killed Jesus on the cross—the Lord raised Him up again! Whatever punishment the high priest could inflict, it was not permanent. But the Holy

Spirit was testifying that what God was doing through them was permanent—eternal.

Friend, I hope you are inspired by the example of the disciples, because I certainly am. Consider the millions of people who came to know Jesus because those disciples were faithful and counted obedience to God more important than their fear of man. In fact, if you think about it, you and I are saved today because they did not give up testifying to the truth. Certainly, we are beneficiaries because they stood strong. They reaped later than they sowed—and we are the fruit of their obedience.

REMEMBER WHOM YOU SERVE

Likewise, we do not have to worry about the consequences when we are doing what God has called us to do. We have to worry about them only when we are *not* obeying Him.

After all, remember whom it is we serve! We covered this briefly when we discussed our convictions about God, but it is truly central to our standing strong in trust and obedience.

First, you can trust God to lead you in the right way and take care of the consequences because *He is omnipotent.* You don't ever have to worry that the Lord will fall short in whatever He asks you to do. He is all-powerful—greater in might than every other force in this universe, including all of them put together. That means none can defeat Him, which in turn means none can overcome you. He is the supreme authority over all that exists, doing whatever He wishes. As Psalm 103:19 reminds us, "The Lord has established His throne in the heavens, and His sovereignty rules over all" (Luke 1:37). No matter how great the trials or obstacles you face, they are as nothing to Him. He is Ruler over them.

And because the Lord is omnipotent, you can be confident that even the enemies you face, the challenges that seem to undermine His purposes, or the trials that dishearten you are actually what He is using supernaturally to fulfill His plans for your life.

Second, you can trust God to lead you in the right way and take care of the consequences because *He is omniscient*. The Lord knows everything and is mind-bogglingly wise, beyond anything we can imagine. So you never have to worry about His being short-sighted or something in your life catching Him by surprise. On the contrary, His understanding extends far into the future. This is because the Lord our God is outside of time. In Isaiah 46:9–10, He says, "I am God, and there is no one like Me, declaring the end from the beginning, and from ancient times things which have not been done, saying, 'My purpose will be established, and I will accomplish all My good pleasure.'"

You and I view time differently from the way He does. When we hear His promises, we think, *That is in the future*. But the Father has already seen their completion and is simply telling us what He has already achieved. Likewise, because of His great knowledge, He is intimately aware of every detail about you—your likes, dislikes, personality, talents, dreams, weaknesses, and desires. This includes your past wounds and struggles, present fears and trials, and what His goal is for creating you. The Lord knows exactly what is going on in every situation that concerns you—even those circumstances that are yet to be. And for each and every one of them, He is preparing you. So even in those troubles that seem to blindside you and send you reeling, trust He knows the best way to lead you.

Also, you can trust God to lead you in the right way and take care of the consequences because *He is omnipresent.* The Lord is everywhere at all times. There is never a time when He has left your side or abandoned you. You are never outside His reach or ability to help you. In fact, God encompasses the whole creation. Everything that exists is constantly and consistently in His presence, regardless of whether it is a

> *T*he Lord knows exactly what is going on in every situation that concerns you—even those circumstances that are yet to be.

place on Earth or a galaxy in the universe that no human technology will ever be able to photograph. He sees it all continually. God is where you cannot be, always working for your benefit and accomplishing His plans for you.

Finally, you can trust God to lead you in the right way and take care of the consequences because *He is omnibenevolent.* The Lord is all-good and unconditionally loving toward you. You may be thinking, *Love? That is not as important as God's omnipotence, omniscience, and omnipresence.* But it absolutely is, because His love is integral to His character. If God acted out of anything other than holy love for you, then you could never be sure whether He was acting in your best interest (Rom. 8:28). But because of His perfect, unconditional love, you know not only that the Father *can* help you, but you can also be certain *He will.*

THE BUILDING PROCESS

Do you believe all of this? Do you truly have confidence that God is all-powerful and all-knowing, that everything is in His presence, and that He loves you perfectly? What you believe will shape your life and influence whether or not you obey the Lord. But the better you know Him, His attributes, and His ways, the more confidence you'll have to trust and obey Him.

This is because trust and obedience work together. The more you trust the Father, the easier it is to obey Him. The more you obey Him, the easier it is to trust Him. These two important areas of our Christian life work together like steps. It is a progressive process in our spiritual growth.

Romans 1:17 talks about the process: "The righteousness of God is revealed from faith to faith; as it is written, 'But the righteous man shall live by faith.'" In other words, God knows your limitations, so He stretches your trust in Him step-by-step—in greater measure each time.

We can see an illustration of this in the life of the prophet Daniel.

Step 1: The test of vegetables.

When Daniel was a teenager, King Nebuchadnezzar invaded Jerusalem and deported him to Babylon (Daniel 1). Along with other bright and promising Hebrew captives, Daniel and three of his friends were selected to train for special service to Nebuchadnezzar. This meant undergoing a rigorous process of assimilation into the Babylonian culture, which included eating

Babylonian food. Unfortunately, the king's cuisine had not been prepared according to Jewish dietary customs and may have been offered to idols, which was strictly forbidden by the Law. So Daniel knew they couldn't eat the king's food and honor God at the same time.

Risking punishment, Daniel asked the commander for permission to eat only vegetables for ten days. The commander expressed his reluctance: "I am afraid of my lord the king, who has appointed your food and your drink; for why should he see your faces looking more haggard than the youths who are your own age? Then you would make me forfeit my head to the king" (v. 10).

But Daniel replied, "Please test your servants for ten days, and let us be given some vegetables to eat and water to drink. Then let our appearance be observed in your presence and the appearance of the youths who are eating the king's choice food; and deal with your servants according to what you see" (vv. 12–13).

Would you say that took faith? I would. If for whatever reason they looked the same as or worse than the other young men being trained, they could have endured some form of retribution from the commander.

Of course, we know that God honored his faith. After those ten days, Daniel and his friends looked better than all the others who had eaten Nebuchadnezzar's food. Likewise, God blessed him with great wisdom and insight. Verse 17 testifies, "God gave them knowledge and intelligence in every branch of literature and wisdom; Daniel even understood all kinds of visions and dreams." This indubitably became a very handy gift when King Nebuchadnezzar had a dream (Daniel 2).

Step 2: The test of dream interpretation.

Scripture reports that in the second year of his reign, Nebuchadnezzar sent for the magicians, conjurers, and sorcerers of his court and said, "I had a dream and my spirit is anxious to understand the dream" (v. 3). However, when they requested he recount it, he replied, "If you do not make known to me the dream and its interpretation, you will be torn limb from limb and your houses will be made a rubbish heap."

His counselors were dumbfounded. How could they interpret a dream if the king did not tell them what was in it? They had no answer for him. When they told the king that his command was impossible to carry out, Nebuchadnezzar ordered that all the wise men of Babylon be executed—including Daniel (vv. 12–13).

Daniel heard of the death sentence and asked the king for time to consult the Lord (v. 16). Would you say this was an even greater test of Daniel's trust in God? I would, because this was not just about what he would eat or whether he faced punishment; this test was about life and death. Daniel had absolutely no control. If the Father did not provide both the dream and the interpretation, they would all be executed.

Thankfully, Daniel 2:26–29 reports:

The king said to Daniel . . . "Are you able to make known to me the dream which I have seen and its interpretation?" Daniel answered before the king and said, "As for the mystery about which the king has inquired, neither wise men, conjurers, magicians nor diviners are able to declare it to the king. *However, there is a God in heaven who reveals mysteries,* and He has made known to King Nebuchadnezzar what will take place in the latter days. This was your dream and the visions in your mind while on your bed. As for you, O king, while on your bed your thoughts turned to what would take place in the future; and He who reveals mysteries has made known to you what will take place" (emphasis added).

That dream was no secret to God. The omnipotent, omniscient, omnipresent, omnibenevolent Lord revealed the vision and its interpretation to Daniel and saved him. And because he trusted God, Daniel rose in the ranks of those wise men. Verse 48 tells us, "Then the king promoted Daniel and gave him many great gifts, and he made him ruler over the whole province of Babylon and chief prefect over all the wise men of Babylon."

Step 3: The test of faithfulness.

Sometime later, the Medo-Persians conquered the Babylonians. As often happened in the ancient world, when one empire overthrew another, the counselors would be assimilated into the new kingdom. In this case, Daniel and the others eventually became advisers to the Persian king Darius. Daniel 6:3 testifies that again, "Daniel began distinguishing himself among the commissioners and satraps because he possessed an extraordinary spirit, and the king planned to appoint him over the entire kingdom."

Not surprisingly, the other counselors and wise men became very jealous of Daniel, and they tried to find a way to trap him and get rid of him. However, because of Daniel's godly character, they had a difficult time of it. They said, "We will not find any ground of accusation against this Daniel unless we find it against him with regard to the law of his God" (v. 5).

They knew it was Daniel's practice to pray three times a day. So they asked King Darius to "give orders that for the next thirty days any person who prays to anyone, divine or human—except to you, Your Majesty—will be thrown into the den of lions" (v. 7 NLT). They targeted the very core of Daniel's relationship with God.

All Daniel had to do was forfeit his prayer time for thirty days and he would be just fine. But if he prayed, he would be fed to the lions.

Think about it: All Daniel had to do was forfeit his prayer time for thirty days and he would be just fine. But if he prayed, he would be fed to the lions. No doubt this was an even greater test of his faith than the others. He had to make a choice: *Is my time alone with God really essential? Is He more important to me than my own life? Would missing my moments with the Lord be more detrimental to me than the ravaging jaws of lions?*

Daniel 6:10 reveals his stunning response: "When Daniel knew that the document was signed, he entered his house . . . and he continued kneeling on his knees three times a day, praying and giving thanks before his God, as he had been doing previously."

What courageous faith! Just consider the reasons most people miss their prayer time. They get busy with other things or just don't count it as that important. To Daniel, his relationship with God was so crucial that not even a death sentence could stop him.

So they threw Daniel in with the lions.

And the Lord delivered him.

CAN GOD TRUST YOU?

Each of Daniel's trials built his obedience to God by stretching his trust in Him. His trust and obedience worked together. Did the Lord stop the trouble from reaching Daniel? No, He did not. But He closed the mouths of those lions.

What I want you to see is that each one of those trials, in increasing measure, taught Daniel to keep his focus on the Lord rather than the circumstances. Because Daniel was loyal and devoted at each step, God increasingly entrusted him with more. In fact, the Lord gave Daniel one of the most illuminating prophecies in Scripture—the vision of the seventy weeks, which we read in Daniel 9:24–27.

Historians have studied those seventy weeks for years and have found that the first part of Daniel's prophecy was fulfilled *to the exact day*: "From the issuing of a decree to restore and rebuild Jerusalem until Messiah the Prince there will be seven weeks and sixty-two weeks." These 69 weeks (or 69 groups of 7) were symbolic of years (483 years in total). By the Jewish calendar, each year would be composed of 360 days. In other words, from the time when Artaxerxes Longimanus decreed to rebuild Jerusalem (on March 14, 445 B.C.) until the Messiah arrived in Jerusalem would be 173,880 days (483 years multiplied by 360 days per year).

Only one Person fits this time frame exactly—Jesus of Nazareth. Exactly 173,880 days after the decree to build Jerusalem, Jesus rode into Jerusalem as Messiah and King—just as was recorded and reported by Daniel (Matt. 21:1–11).

The Lord could trust Daniel with that information.

But the real question is: *Can God trust you?*

Will you trust and obey God regardless of what He calls you to do? When the lions of everyday life seem to close in on you, will you continue to believe in God, trust His character, and obey Him?

Remember, "Without faith it is impossible to please Him, for he who comes to God must believe that He is and that He is a rewarder of those who seek Him." Will you say with your life: "I believe that God exists and I have confidence that He is a rewarder of those who seek Him"?

Because you see, the very challenge before you today is a stepping-stone to the greater things the Father wants to do through you. So whatever you're facing, obey God and leave the consequences to Him. It will cause you to grow in a manner that honors the Lord, and what you will reap will certainly be worthwhile.

7

YOUR CONVICTIONS ABOUT GOD, PART 3

The Holy Spirit: Is It His Life
That's Pouring Out of You?

*P*erhaps after the last chapter, you're thinking, *I love Jesus and want to follow Him, but I am certainly no Daniel and I am not at all like the apostles. They were called to that kind of life—I'm not. God couldn't possibly do through me what He did through them. I'm not even sure I'd want Him to if He could!*

But understand, in order to live a Christian life that can weather the storms, you need to allow Jesus to live *His* life in and through you. Yes, the Lord calls some into active ministry, and that may not be you. But the Lord calls *everyone* to be a fully participating member of His Body—His dynamic presence in the world.

You have the potential to be the channel through which God affects this whole world through your testimony, prayers, and service. Just think of the examples we've had throughout history.

At the age of eighteen, after being turned down for many jobs, a young man was able to get only a position at his uncle's shoe store. He was uneducated, his English was poor, and he probably didn't think much of himself. But after Jesus got hold of him, that fellow, Dwight L. Moody, became one of the nineteenth century's greatest evangelists.

But rather than focusing on Moody, let's think about the man who led him to the Lord. Edward Kimball was a Sunday school teacher who simply had a heart to serve Jesus. The lonely teenager Dwight Moody was one of his students. One day Kimball decided to come to the shoe store and share Christ more completely with Dwight. Do you think Kimball looked at Moody and said, "Here's a fellow who's going to be a famous evangelist. I think I'll talk to him"? No. Kimball was just one man speaking to a student about what Jesus had done to save him. But Kimball had an incredible impact on Moody—and therefore the world—because he was faithful. As I said in the previous chapter, don't ever underestimate what God can do with your acts of obedience.

Likewise, it is estimated that the great Charles Haddon Spurgeon preached to approximately ten million people, even though he did not have the modern-day conveniences of radio and television to help broadcast his sermons. To this day, he remains a widely read author, even though he died in January 1892. You would think that with that kind of influence, the person who led him to the Lord must have been an important Christian leader. But nothing could be further from the truth.

In fact, the day C. H. Spurgeon accepted Jesus as his Savior, it had snowed so much that the pastor could not make it to the church. Spurgeon had heard many noteworthy people preach, but none of them answered the most profound question of his heart: "How can I get my sins forgiven?"[2] But on that day, with no pastor present and no more than fifteen people braving the snow to worship in that small Primitive Methodist chapel, someone agreed to give the message. Spurgeon writes,

> At last, a very thin-looking man, a shoemaker, or tailor, or something of that sort, went up into the pulpit to preach. Now, it is well that preachers should be instructed; but this man was really stupid. He was obliged to stick to his text, for the simple reason that he had little else to say. The text was,—"LOOK UNTO ME, AND BE YE SAVED, ALL THE ENDS OF THE EARTH."
>
> He did not even pronounce the words rightly, but that did not matter. There was, I thought, a glimpse of hope for me in that text . . . When he had . . . managed to spin out ten minutes or so, he was at the end of his tether.
>
> Then he looked at me under the gallery, and I daresay, with so few present, he knew me to be a stranger. Just fixing his eyes on me, as if he knew all my heart, he said, "Young man, you look very miserable." Well, I did; but I had not been accustomed to have remarks made from the pulpit on my personal appearance before. However, it was a good blow, struck right home.
>
> He continued, "and you always will be miserable—miserable in life, and miserable in death,—if you don't obey my text; but if you obey now, this moment, you will be saved." Then, lifting up his hands, he shouted, as only a Primitive Methodist could do, "Young man, look to Jesus Christ. Look! Look! Look! You have nothin' to do but to look and live."

I saw at once the way of salvation . . . I had been waiting to do fifty things, but when I heard that word, "Look!" what a charming word it seemed to me! Oh! I looked until I could almost have looked my eyes away. There and then the cloud was gone, the darkness had rolled away, and that moment I saw the sun; and I could have risen that instant, and sung with the most enthusiastic of them, of the precious blood of Christ, and the simple faith which looks alone to Him.[3]

It was not the cleverness or the brilliance of the message that captured Spurgeon's attention. On the contrary, Spurgeon's testimony was that the man was less gifted in the area of intellect and oratory than many others he had heard. Rather, it was the power of God through His Word that spoke to Spurgeon in such a profound way.

We may not know too much about the man who led C. H. Spurgeon to Christ. But what we do know is that because he was faithful, the Lord changed the landscape of eternity for many people.

The same can be true for you. Whether you are called into the ministry like Moody or Spurgeon, or are simply living in obedience to the Father like Kimball or that Primitive Methodist fellow, your success doesn't rely on your talents, genius, or charm. It all depends on the power of the living God flowing in and through you. And the lasting impact you can make defies imagination.

THE POWER WE BUILD ON

Of course, we have been talking about how we build on the foundation of our lives in order to stand strong. As we discussed in the previous chapter, when we come before God, He will "stretch" our faith—asking us to trust Him and obey Him in situations that are far beyond us. In that way, He builds our trust and faith in Him and leads us to accomplish His goals—purposes that have enduring value (1 Cor. 3:12–13).

Naturally, one of the reasons we become fearful is that we measure the enormity of what the Lord calls us to do against our own meager abilities and resources. Whatever challenge is before you today may be a case in point. You don't feel prepared enough to go forward. Perhaps you doubt your capabilities, your supplies are scarce, your strength is diminished, or your time is too constrained. You fear that you will fail, that people will laugh at you, or that you will be hurt.

This is because our natural tendency is to think that we are completely responsible for what the Lord calls us to do. In other words, we think of ministry as *our* work *for* God. But the truth of the matter is that we are not even able to live the Christian life in our own strength. We can feel completely helpless to change our own hearts—forget anyone else's. We know the fallen, sinful, weak, inadequate people we are, so how can we possibly make an impact for the Kingdom of God? Even though we may genuinely want to serve the Lord,

Our natural tendency is to think that we are completely responsible for what the Lord calls us to do.

no matter how diligently we try, we keep slipping back into the same bad habits and feel like we're falling short of all He has for us (Rom. 7:14–15).

But the good news is that *you were never meant to live the Christian life in your own strength.* The true Christian life is not so much that you live *for* Jesus—how is that approach any different from a person devoting himself or herself to any other religion or cause? Rather, the Christian life is Jesus living *through* you, and you are thus empowered to do the work only He can do.

Remember, the Father never asks you to do anything for Him with only your own strength. No, friend, He has chosen you for the tasks and challenges before you so He can shine His power through you—so that when the work is accomplished, people won't look to you, *they will look to Him* (1 Cor. 1:25–31).

Just think about the disciples. They were largely uneducated, simple men. They had no extraordinary skills, resources, or strategic value on their own. So when Jesus said, "Go therefore and make disciples of all the nations, baptizing them in the name of the Father and the Son and the Holy Spirit, teaching them to observe all that I commanded you" (Matt. 28:19–20), He certainly realized they were completely incapable of taking the Good News of salvation to the whole world by themselves. But then, no one would ever say that the influence, the spread, or the endurance of the gospel was because of those disciples. Rather, it is the power of God that fuels it.

That is why the emphasis of Christ's Great Commission *begins and ends with Christ's power and presence.* Jesus told them, "All authority has been given to Me in heaven and on earth . . . and lo, I am with you always, even to the end of the age" (Matt. 28:18–20).

The reason the gospel continues to transform lives today is that God Himself empowers it.

Only by learning to rely on Jesus could that handful of believers obey the command to take the Good News to the world (Acts 4:13). The same is true for us—anything we do for the Father *must begin and end with His power and presence.*

BEING A WILLING VESSEL

This is why brokenness is God's requirement for maximum usefulness. We must come to the point where we understand that our ability is always inadequate and insufficient. Only the power of God at work in and through us can move mountains (2 Cor. 12:9–10). When we stop relying on ourselves and instead rely on the Lord, we can do anything.

This is the concept we find in John 15:5, when Jesus said, "I am the vine, you are the branches; he who abides in Me and I in him, he bears much fruit, for apart from Me you can do nothing." How does a natural branch attached to a vine bear fruit? There is no need for it to do anything, of course; it simply grows. As long as that branch is attached to the vine, it is fed, nourished, and given everything needed for life.

Sadly, most believers are like branches that strain to produce fruit by our own virtue and strength. No wonder we get so frustrated. But this is the case throughout all of Scripture; it has always been and always will be God who does the work through us.

Consider Moses (Exod. 1–17). Did he take it upon himself to deliver the people of Israel from bondage in Egypt? No, it was the Great I Am who called him, saying, "I have surely seen the affliction of My people who are in Egypt . . . So I have come down to deliver them from the power of the Egyptians" (Exod. 3:7–8).

Did Moses have to come up with a way to save the Hebrews or to convince Pharaoh to let them go? No, God had it all figured out; He had already planned the plagues (Exod. 7:1–5).

Did Moses have to turn the water into blood? Did he gather the frogs, gnats, insects, or locusts, or do anything else to bring about the plagues the Lord had spoken of? Of course not. God performed all those signs and wonders (Exod. 7:14–11:10).

Was Moses required to part the Red Sea on his own? No, that was far beyond his abilities, but the Father did it faithfully. In fact, Moses told the people, "Do not fear! Stand by and see the salvation of the Lord *which He will accomplish* for you today; for the Egyptians whom you have seen today, you will never see them again forever. *The Lord will fight for you* while you keep silent" (Exod. 14:13–14; emphasis added).

But surely Moses had to have a strategy for defeating the Egyptian army once the people of Israel had gotten past the Red Sea, didn't he? No. God allowed the towering waters of the sea to swallow their chariots as they pursued the Hebrews.

How about directions or a map? Of all things, Moses certainly needed to know where he was going, right? Actually, no. The Lord led them by a pillar of cloud by day and a pillar of fire by night to give them light and protection (Exod. 13:21–22).

How about food? Did Moses have to plan and acquire all the food for that multitude of Hebrews? Absolutely not. Even in this, the Lord God was faithful. He provided water, manna, and quail for them as they traveled (Exod. 15:22–16:18).

Are you getting the picture? Of course, you may be thinking, *Surely Moses had to do something.* Yes, he did—*he abided in God.* He stayed close to the Lord, listened to Him, obeyed, and remained a willing vessel for all of God's plans.

It is not by our efforts, but by the unhindered life of Jesus flowing through us by faith that His Kingdom work is accomplished.

And that is what we are called to do as well. It is not by our efforts, but by the unhindered life of Jesus flowing through us by faith that His Kingdom work is accomplished. What we have been called to is *His* life, *His* purposes, *His* ministry, *His* fruit—not our own.

THINKING WE NEED TO KNOW

Being a willing vessel of God's work is easier said than done, of course. Although this is the life we are called to live, it is by no means natural to us. The Father asks us to walk with Him in faith, but when the storms arise, our ordinary inclination is to cry out, "Lord, shouldn't there be a plan?" Obviously, God has one and it will be successful, but when we don't know what it is, we doubt Him. We think we need to know the end plan before we move forward, but that's not the case.

Like the disciples who were caught in the storm while Jesus slept in the stern of the boat, we cry out, "Teacher, do You not care that we are perishing?" (Mark 4:38). We know now that nothing was going to happen to that vessel because Jesus still had to go to the cross and rise from the grave. Likewise, those disciples were safe because the Lord was going to work through them to spread the Good News of salvation all over the world. But we have the luxury of hindsight—they didn't know any such thing. So until Jesus "rebuked the wind and said to the sea, 'Hush, be still'" (Mark 4:39), they remained in their fear.

Often, we do as well. We want to know God's plan for us—not one step at a time but all of it at once—especially when adversity arises that doesn't make sense to us. However, we miss the fact that the very definition of walking by faith means trusting the Lord to lead us inch by inch and mile by mile, despite the challenges that arise along the way.

Unfortunately, feeling vulnerable and without recourse, we come up with our own plans and ask God to bless them. This is the repeated temptation when we walk with the Father. When we do, these consequences follow:

+ We fall short of our potential, missing the very purposes for which God created us.

+ We feel incomplete.

+ We waste time.

+ We experience the burnout and futility of relying solely on our own strength and wisdom.

+ What we do is only temporal; it passes away. Because really, apart from Christ, we can do nothing of eternal value.

Friend, God wants us to walk in complete faith of His love, power, wisdom, and provision. And we can be assured He will reveal His plans to us and give us the joy of being part of His work—which is far greater, more fulfilling, more energizing, more fruitful, and more eternity shaking than anything we could ever possibly come up with on our own.

So going back to John 15:5, our work as a branch is not to come up with our own plans but to seek out God's (James 4:13–15)—regardless of how our circumstances look—because everything He does succeeds and has eternal value. And if the Father has not yet revealed the next step, we wait for Him in confidence, sure He will not let us down.

A DIFFERENT LIFE ALTOGETHER

Although the apostle Paul had once persecuted followers of the crucified Christ, he came to say, "I have been crucified with Christ; and it is no longer I who live, but Christ lives in me; and the life which I now live in the flesh I live by faith in the Son of God, who loved me and gave Himself up for me" (Gal. 2:20). Paul understood that the only life of eternal impact—the only life worth living—was the life of Christ expressed through him and the purposes for which God had created him.

We must not miss the significance of what Paul said: *I have been crucified with Christ; and it is no longer I who live.* Crucifixion is death. We are to count our own life and will as lost. What Paul is saying is that we must be like Jesus—we must go to the cross willingly (Rom. 8:29). We must allow the execution of our own ways. But we do not do so in a fatalistic way. No, we do so in order to experience a *better* life—that we may attain the indestructible, victorious resurrected life (Phil. 3:8–11).

Christ lives in me. Not your life—*His*. Not your energy, might, or wisdom—*His*. This takes trust not only that the life Jesus offers you is far superior to the one you can live on your own, but also that He is *able* to clean out your old self and truly make something new, worthwhile, and powerful of you (2 Cor. 5:17).

How do we do this? Trusting in God, accepting His life, and having confidence in His complete provision is a discipline of surrender we must learn.

Thankfully, the God who saved you is the One who instructs you. If you can trust Him to forgive you of your sins and give you eternal life, then you can be certain He will teach you how to allow His life to flow through you.

God seals you with His Holy Spirit at salvation, and His Spirit lives in you until the day of redemption (Eph. 1:13–14). The Holy Spirit is the Lord's constant presence with us, indwelling us for the purpose of blessing, enabling, energizing, equipping, guiding, healing, informing, transforming, warning us, and producing eternal fruit through us.

Let's look once again at John 15:5, where Jesus said, "I am the vine, you are the branches; he who abides in Me and I in him, he bears much fruit, for apart from Me you can do nothing." It might help to think of the Holy Spirit as the sap that runs from the vine to the branch—from God to us—giving us all the divine, supernatural nutrients we need to generate the fruit we were created to yield. He is the resurrection-life of Christ in us. Our need to know the specifics of the Lord's plan is nowhere near

The Holy Spirit gives us all the divine, supernatural nutrients we need to generate the fruit we were created to yield.

as great as our need to understand all that He has given us through His presence. The Holy Spirit

- *enables us*—helping us to do everything God calls us to do, engineering our circumstances for His purposes.

- *energizes us*—giving us the vitality, endurance, and strength for the tasks He calls us to accomplish, so we don't give up when times are tough.

- *equips us*—giving us His wisdom, giftedness, and resources for every part of His plan.

- *guides us*—showing us how to proceed step-by-step and assuring us that we are never alone.

- *heals us*—curing us of the wounds within us, which nothing in this world can overcome except His wonderful presence.

- *informs us*—teaching us what we need to know when we need to know it.

- *transforms us*—conforming us to the likeness of Christ. We can try to produce the fruit of the Spirit—love, joy, peace, patience, kindness, goodness, faithfulness, gentleness, and self-control (Gal. 5:22–23)—on our own, but we never get very far. No, it has to be God producing that in us.

- *warns us*—alerting us to the pitfalls of sin and traps of the enemy.

- *produces eternal fruit through us*—generating a harvest in our own lives and in the lives of others that will last forever.

The Holy Spirit is always at hand to enable us with counsel, strength, and any form of help that we require. In fact, God assumes *full responsibility* for our needs when we obey Him so that the assignment can be accomplished in the manner that brings Him maximum glory.

DIVINE PROVISION AND SUPERNATURAL EMPOWERING

We see examples of the Spirit-enabled resurrection-life in the stories of great men of faith who knew God would come through for them. Like George Müller, a nineteenth-century pastor who founded 117 Christian schools and started many orphanages in England, despite the fact he had no money. He and the matrons of the houses often found themselves without the resources to feed the orphans, but the Lord always provided for their needs in extraordinary ways. For example, on one occasion, Müller wrote,

> Never were we so reduced in funds as to-day. There was not a single halfpenny in hand between the matrons of the three houses . . . for none of the houses had we the prospect of being able to take in bread. When I left the brethren and sisters at one o'clock, after prayer, I told them that we must wait for help, and see how the Lord would deliver us this time. *I was sure of help*, but we were indeed straitened. When I came to Kingsdown, I felt that I needed more exercise, being very cold; wherefore I went not the nearest way home, but round by Clarence Place. About twenty yards from my house, I met a brother who walked back with me,

and after a little conversation gave me £10 to be handled over to the brethren, the deacons, towards providing the poor saints with coals, blankets and warm clothing; also £5 for the Orphans, and £5 for the other objects of the Scriptural Knowledge Institution. The brother had called twice while I was gone to the Orphan-Houses, and had I now been one half minute later, I should have missed him. *But the Lord knew our need, and therefore allowed me to meet him.*[4]

This may seem a simple example in a world where food is so readily available. But this man was trusting God for three houses full of children who would have starved without the Lord's provision. Do not miss how in His exact and perfect timing, He ordained Müller's steps. God was leading Müller even when he was not fully aware of it (Phil. 2:13). Again and again, Müller and the orphans seemed at the edge of disaster with no way to help themselves, but the Father faithfully supplied their needs each and every time. Müller got to the point where he was no longer reliant on the resources of earth because the storehouses of heaven had been opened to him and provided exactly as he needed (Deut. 8:16–18).

But it is not only in divine provision that the Holy Spirit enables us, but also by supernatural empowering. For example, in the early 1900s, pastor Watchman Nee and several Christian brothers went to witness to a village on the island of Mei-Hwa off of the Chinese coast. None of the inhabitants showed any interest in what they had to say about Jesus.

Nee's companion, Brother Wu, asked, "Why will none of you believe?" Nee reports:

Someone in the crowd replied at once, "We have a god—one god—Ta-wang, and he has never failed us. He is an effective god." "How do you know that you can trust him?" asked Wu. "We have held his festival procession every January for 286 years. The chosen day is revealed by divination beforehand, and every year without fail his day is a perfect one without rain or cloud," was the reply. "When is the procession this year?" "It is fixed for January 11 at eight in the morning." "Then," said brother Wu impetuously, "I promise you that it will certainly rain on the eleventh." At once there was an outburst of cries from the crowd. "That is enough! We don't want to hear any more preaching. If there is rain on the eleventh, then your God is God!"[5]

So Nee, Wu, and the brothers devoted themselves to prayer, asking God to provide the miracle.

However, pause a moment and put yourself in Nee's shoes in this particular instance. A young brother in the faith has just promised that there would be rain on a day that had not seen precipitation for almost three hundred years. Even the most seasoned and informed meteorologist would be loath to make such a forecast. Not only is your credibility as a witness for Christ on the line, but so is whether or not the twenty-thousand-plus people on that island believe in Him for salvation. And who knew how those villagers would retaliate against them if the day came and went without rain. Had that incredible prediction been God's will or Brother Wu's recklessness?

In other words, if any of us were in this same situation, the doubts and fears would flood in. We would recognize the precariousness of the situation—the immense danger of failure and how out of control we really are. Perhaps we believe God *could* bring the rain—we trust in His *ability* to do so. However, we might not be sure He actually *wants to*. We would question if we had said and done the right things, whether there was any sin blocking His power from flowing, or any way we fall short that displeases Him. Likewise, we might wonder about Ta-wang's powers. Maybe we've seen so much evil in the world that we're uncertain God will actually intervene.

I imagine the same was true for Nee. He wrote, "We asked the Lord to forgive us if we had overstepped ourselves. I tell you, we were in deadly earnest. What had we done? Had we made a terrible mistake, or dare we ask God for a miracle? . . . What should we do? Should we leave now?"[6]

It is important to understand that the difference between the Spirit-enabled person and the one who isn't is not that there is no longer fear or doubt. Rather, the person who has the life of Christ in him or her is the one who does not run away from what the Lord is doing but waits for Him to reveal the next step. A Spirit-enabled person stands firm while others fail because of the supernatural determination of God in him or her.

Even Nee asked, "Should we leave now?" But he kept listening to the Father. He wrote, "Up to this point we had feared to pray for rain. Then, like a flash, there came the word to me, 'Where is the God of Elijah?' It came with such clarity and power that I knew it was from God. Confidently I announced

A Spirit-enabled person stands firm while others fail because of the supernatural determination of God in him or her.

to the brothers, 'I have the answer. The Lord will send rain on the eleventh.'"[7]

Of course, Nee was referring to the fact that the prophet Elijah prayed for rain after three years of drought and the Lord answered His prayer (1 Kings 18:41–46). Nee didn't take the word that came to him as a passing thought or his imagination run amok. He accepted that word in faith as did his companions. So they continued to pray and testify to the truth of the gospel.

Finally, January 11 arrived, and Nee woke up about an hour before the festival was due to begin. His heart sank when he saw the sun shining and not a cloud in the sky. The villagers ran about getting ready to worship Ta-wang. Nee's friends gathered for breakfast—still absolutely no sign of rain in sight—and they offered a short prayer of faith—grateful to the Lord for sending a shower in time.

Before they were able to say, "Amen," the raindrops started hitting the roof. By the time they'd finished their breakfast, a downpour was inundating the street. Outside, they could hear some of the villagers yelling, "There is God; there is no Ta-wang! He is kept in by the rain!"[8]

Yes, You Too

Like the prophet Elijah, Nee and his companions experienced a supernatural empowering, provision, and enabling that defies explanation. So you see, these miracles didn't happen only in ancient times—they continue today. This is possible *for you*! This is what is available to you and me as we submit to God daily. And this is the understanding that should set us free us to accept all that the Father calls us to do with joy and confidence—knowing we will see and experience His extraordinary provision if we believe in Him.

However, this also requires us to understand that the Holy Spirit does not exist to empower *our* plans; rather, He carries out *God's* purposes through us. Pastor and evangelist R. A. Torrey reminds us, "The Holy Spirit is not merely a divine power that we get hold of and use according to our will, but . . . is a divine Person who gets hold of us and uses us according to His will."[9]

God's ways are not our ways. His plans are always much grander, more far-reaching, and more profound than our own. We would not necessarily *choose* the challenges He allows in our lives, because they

The Holy Spirit does not exist to empower our *plans; rather, He carries out* God's *purposes through us.*

are out of our control and beyond our understanding. Certainly, Watchman Nee and his companions would have preferred to lead the people of Mei-Hwa to the Lord in a way that didn't require the divine provision of rain. Likewise, I am sure George Müller would have preferred to have plenty of money to feed his orphans rather than be so reliant upon God's supernatural intervention.

Yet those were the very places where they experienced the glory of God and His life flowing through them!

In fact, Müller said, "If we desire our faith to be strengthened, we should not shrink from opportunities where our faith may be tried, and therefore, through trial, be strengthened." If you truly want to be a person who stands strong, you cannot avoid the challenges God gives you because they build the greatest resource in you: faith in the Lord—His very life flowing through you.

Because God's plans are so far outside our grasp, they remind us that the responsibility for the Lord's work is *supposed to be* in His hands because only He really understands people's hearts and what it is they sincerely yearn for. Only He can identify and supply their deepest needs. Only He has resurrection power! On our own, we can never truly fulfill God's plan. It would be as impossible for us as calling rain down from the sky by ourselves.

Even today the challenges and opportunities you're facing may very well be far beyond your gifts, talents, time, or reach. Good! This way, you can know for certain God is calling you to step out in faith and stand strong for Him.

Friend, know for certain you can do it without being afraid. *Say it out loud*: "This is supposed to be bigger than I am so that I will rely upon You, my Lord and my God. So Jesus, let Your life flow through me! I place my trust in You completely."

Give yourself over to Him, and you'll be amazed at all He does through you.

THE HOW OF RELYING ON GOD

How do you do it? How do you rely on God to do things that are beyond your ability?

First, admit that living the Christian life is not something you can do on your own.

Let go. This is often the most difficult part, because the pride that lives within us will fight against it. We don't want to admit that we are weak or that we are unable to do something. Putting our trust in God's hands makes us feel vulnerable, out of control, and perhaps even irresponsible. Instead, we prefer to be recognized for our talents and what a wonderful job we've done. We want to do things our way and have people praise us for it.

Unfortunately, that means that we are focused on ourselves rather than on God. However, admitting that we are inadequate liberates us in profound ways. Then we will say, "Lord, I am Your servant. Work through me to glorify Yourself." This centers our attention on God rather than on our service and opens us to what the Lord of all Creation can accomplish.

> *Admitting that we are inadequate liberates us in profound ways.*

Second, thank God for your inadequacies.

Voice your gratitude for those things that keep you humble and dependent upon Him. Understand that your Creator put those limitations in your life *for the very purpose of liberating you* from your dependence on yourself. Your shortcomings are what keep you close to the Father and allow you to know Him better. Since you can't help yourself in those areas, your only recourse is to rest in Jesus and allow Him to do all the work through you.

The truth of the matter is that our successes can be our downfall if we become prideful about them. Recall what Paul wrote in 2 Corinthians 12:7–10:

> Because of the surpassing greatness of the revelations, for this reason, to keep me from exalting myself, there was given me a thorn in the flesh, a messenger of Satan to torment me—to keep me from exalting myself! Concerning

this I implored the Lord three times that it might leave me. And He has said to me, "My grace is sufficient for you, for power is perfected in weakness." Most gladly, therefore, I will rather boast about my weaknesses, so that the power of Christ may dwell in me. Therefore I am well content with weaknesses, with insults, with distresses, with persecutions, with difficulties, for Christ's sake; for when I am weak, then I am strong.

Paul repeats the reason: Because he had received such incredible revelations, the Lord was making sure he *wouldn't sin by becoming conceited and exalting himself.* Do you recall what those revelations were? At the beginning of 2 Corinthians 12 we learn that Paul had seen the third heaven (v. 2)—the highest heaven, where God's throne is said to reside. He said he "was caught up into Paradise and heard inexpressible words, which a man is not permitted to speak" (v. 4). What an incredible privilege!

After having such close contact with the living God, Paul could have become very arrogant. He knew and understood things no other person had been exposed to—and he could have been tempted to make that the basis of his worth or think himself better than others because of it. But he recognized that the infirmities given to him were for the purpose of keeping him reliant upon God and humble toward others.

That is true for you as well—and it is why you should praise God for your inadequacies. Do not hide them. This is one of the problems in many churches today. Believers try to act "perfect" so that others will think they are "good Christians." They hide their limitations and shortcomings so people will respect them.

Meanwhile, they tout their accomplishments. Perhaps they have been in the church a lengthy amount of time, know some theology, or hold a prominent position in the fellowship—whatever gives them an excuse to feel superior to and look down on others.

But Paul is clear: It is in our weaknesses that we relate to others and through which Christ is exalted. That is where the real ministry and miracles of God take place. So it is wise to thank the Father for them.

Third, acknowledge that Christ is sufficient.

Since He is God, Jesus has the ability to meet every requirement, give you wisdom for every decision, and endow you with strength for every situation. As I said, God assumes full responsibility for your needs when you obey Him.

So set your heart to trust that the Father is in supernatural control of the challenges you face, and give Him permission to live His life through you. Let go of your own efforts to "be a good Christian" or "do enough" to please Him. Surrender any notion that you will win this battle on your own. Instead, whenever the situation seems untenable and the fears overwhelm you, confess it to be true—state out loud, "Jesus, I trust that You will live Your life through me and that You have allowed this as an incredible opportunity for Your glory to shine! Thank You for showing that You are sufficient no matter how profound my need."

Now, just a word of warning on this point—this is not a one-time commitment. We've heard the exhortation of Romans 12:1: "To present your bodies a living and holy sacrifice." But as we all know, the problem with living sacrifices is that they keep crawling off the altar. We are continually tempted to take our lives back.

You will most likely find yourself needing to surrender to God daily (Luke 9:23). In fact, when trials are at their worst, you may find yourself having to submit to Him hour by hour and minute by minute. But do not lose heart or grow frustrated with yourself. Rather, recognize that letting go and allowing Christ to be your life and sufficiency is a very difficult battle, which at times requires your moment-by-moment surrender.

Likewise, when you fail by taking matters back into your own hands, remind yourself that this is simply more evidence that Jesus must empower you. Your ways are insufficient—you cannot live the Christian life on your own; He must live it through you.

Fourth, abide in Christ by continuing to seek God diligently— obeying as He directs you.

Of course, we have discussed all the ways you do so. But as a brief review, it includes:

+ *Meditate on God's Word.* Doing so reminds you who He is, how He has helped people in the past, and how He will continue to help you. Romans 15:4 explains: "Whatever was written in earlier times was written for our instruction, so that through perseverance and the encouragement of the Scriptures we might have hope." Scripture is a constant, consistent testimony that all the ways God empowered Moses, Joshua, Abraham, David, and Paul are available to you as well. All the provision, strength, and wisdom He gave them, He will also provide to you. Likewise, through His Word, He will illuminate problems with what you think and believe (Heb. 4:12) and transform your thoughts (Rom. 12:2).

* *Pray.* Remember, your intimacy with God is key. The Father will speak directly to your heart about every situation. Paul realized that the thorn in his side was from God for his good because he had constant interaction with the Lord. Likewise, the Father will help you to understand what He is working on in you as you keep connected to Him through prayer.

* *Obey God when His directions to you don't make sense.* At times, God will work on areas of your life where there is a stronghold or a blind spot, but you may not immediately understand what He is doing. Obey Him anyway. The Lord does not require you to understand His will, just obey it, even if it seems unreasonable. As Proverbs 3:5–6 instructs, "Trust in the Lord with all your heart and do not lean on your own understanding. In all your ways acknowledge Him, and He will make your paths straight." Remember, this is His life you are living, which requires His wisdom. If your comprehension of the situation causes you to doubt the Lord, then the Father may be indicating that your reliance on your own sense of logic and insight is preventing you from experiencing His life in and through you. When you insist on relying on your own insight, you are, in essence, choosing to place more faith in your capacity to understand than in the Father's ability to lead you. But friend, you do not and cannot know all the details about your situation, but He does. Trust Him to clear the areas where His life needs to flow through you.

Finally, make sure that all you do points others to Christ.

Who is the life of Christ in us? The Holy Spirit. And what does Scripture declare to be the Holy Spirit's role? In John 15:6, Jesus tells us, "When the Helper comes, whom I will send to you from the Father, that is the Spirit of truth who proceeds from the Father, *He will testify about Me*" (emphasis added).

Trust Him to clear the areas where His life needs to flow through you.

When the life of Christ is flowing through us, what we do will lead people to Jesus. That is the divine harvest that is produced when we are fully devoted to Him.

Perhaps you have experienced this without realizing it. People approach you, saying they see something different about you and they want to know what it is.

Or perhaps others seek you out for counsel or comfort. They cannot explain why, but they feel they can count on you even though they don't know you very well.

All the while, what is really happening is that through you, the Holy Spirit is eliciting a desire for Christ in them. This is not because of clever stories or illustrations you've come up with, and it's certainly not dependent upon your personal charisma or popularity. Rather, this is about the living God drawing people to Himself through you (Matt. 5:16). They see Him in your eyes, words, and actions—and they long to experience His presence for themselves, though perhaps they cannot express it in so many words.

This is the natural result of His resurrected life in you. Jesus said, "I, if I am lifted up from the earth, will draw all men to Myself" (John 12:32). When His life is flowing in you, He will be exalted through you. And you'll be amazed at the supernatural way people will commit themselves to Him because of you.

And what is Christ's promise to you through it all? We saw it at the beginning of this chapter. Jesus says, "Lo, I am with you always, even to the end of the age" (Matt. 28:20). Your victorious Savior promises that He will never leave or forsake you. There is no greater guarantee of success than that.

PERSONAL INVENTORY

The truth of the matter is, if you want to achieve something meaningful in this life or the life to come, it is not going to be through your own strength. Everything in this world—every kingdom, every ideology, every human endeavor—eventually comes to an end. There is only One who endures—and that is God Himself— and what He accomplishes by His will and power will also endure. What He establishes will stand strong to the end of this world and in eternity.

The good news is that not only are you invited to partake in it, but God Himself prepares you for it. The key is for you to let Him.

With that in mind, I invite you to spend some time in reflection and repentance. The biggest impediments to the life of Christ flowing through you are the areas that you refuse to give to Him, whether consciously or unintentionally.

Each of us has these places in our lives where we are relying on ourselves rather than on God. We may or may not be aware of what they are. But we have to deal with them when the Father brings them to our attention, so we can continue to grow in our relationship with Him.

Therefore, please take a few minutes to pray as David did: "Search me, O God, and know my heart; try me and know my anxious thoughts; and see if there be any hurtful way in me, and lead me in the everlasting way" (Ps. 139:23–24).

As you wait quietly before Him, deliberately submit your heart to Him.

+ Is there something in your life God is bringing to mind?

+ Is there any sin that you need to confess?

+ Are there areas of inadequacy that keep coming up?

+ Is there someone you need to forgive?

+ Do you have a stronghold of security in your life?

+ Are you refusing to turn over your need for money, sex, political power, control, your reputation, or the need for people to respect you or love you?

+ Are you putting anything before God Himself?

Consider each of the fruits of the Spirit carefully. Do you overflow with

+ love?

+ joy?

+ peace?

+ patience?

+ kindness?

+ goodness?

+ faithfulness?

+ gentleness?

+ self-control?

Are any of these a struggle? Do you feel a significant lack in any of these areas? When the life of Christ is flowing freely through you, these fruits will proceed from you naturally. So if any of these fruits are being impeded in you, be assured it is evidence that there is something God wants to deal with in your life.

Likewise, if you feel angry, fearful, depressed, guilty, bitter, or hopeless, there is bondage from which Jesus desires to liberate you. If you sense the pressure of death bearing down on you—as if you are being crushed under the weight of your burdens—there is something that is stopping you from experiencing the extraordinary, eternal life you were created for, and the Savior is striving to set you free.

Ask God what is impeding His Holy Spirit from having free reign in you. Do not deny *anything* He brings to mind. Even the seemingly random thoughts that arise may very well be something the Lord wants to deal with. Trust Him to give you wisdom and understanding about the walls and wounds that you may not realize are thwarting you.

Ask God what is impeding His Holy Spirit from having free reign in you. Do not deny anything He brings to mind.

The areas you refuse to release are where you are holding on to your limited, frail, perishable life, and where you are forsaking the abundant, indestructible resurrection-life Christ desires for you. So, friend, confess *whatever* it is that the Father reveals to you. Agree with God that it is a problem so you can have freedom, His life can flow through you without any hindrance or reservation, and you will have everything you need to stand strong.

8

YOUR CONVICTIONS ABOUT YOUR ROLE

Self-Serve or Serving Others?

*U*p until now, we have been discussing standing strong and living the Christian life as individuals. This makes sense because Jesus saves us each independently, and we have a *personal* relationship with Him. You cannot claim another person's faith—you must believe in Jesus yourself and set your own heart to trust, obey, and live for Him.

However, as we talk about building a life that stands strong and allowing the life of Christ to flow through us, we cannot ignore the relationships we have with others. As we mentioned earlier, Paul instructs: "If any man builds on the foundation with gold, silver, precious stones, wood, hay, straw, each man's work will become evident; for the day will show it because it is to be revealed with fire, and the fire itself will test the quality of each man's work" (1 Cor. 3:12–13). We know that the gold, silver, and precious stones are the works we do in obedience to God, and the wood, hay, and straw, which burn up, are the self-willed things we do.

What we must also realize, though, is that all of this impacts the people we know as well. In the end, how we build and invest in others will make us either stronger with good, godly, Christ-centered relationships or weaker through self-centered and worldly associations.

Now, everyone will have different relationships, family structures, and challenges. It would be very difficult to cover all of the beliefs that impede or undermine healthy relationships here, although I do cover many of them in my books *Emotions* and *How to Keep Your Kids on Your Team*. I believe that when you submit to God, He will teach you a proper view of yourself and will produce the fruit of the Spirit through you; then you will begin to treat others with greater compassion, love, and respect.

How we build and invest in others will make us either stronger with good, godly, Christ-centered relationships or weaker through self-centered and worldly associations.

However, where I think we often have persistent problems in our beliefs is in regard to our *role*—especially as it relates to God living out His purposes through us. So instead of looking at the *mechanics* of relationships, such as how to communicate well or having boundaries with others, I want to talk more about your *part* in relationships—how God planned for you and me to *fit in* as members of His family.

You see, I encounter more and more people who see no reason to engage with the Body of Christ, preferring instead to know God on their own. I use the term "Body of Christ" purposefully here, because it is used in the New Testament to describe our relationship with others who believe in Jesus. In Romans 12:5, we're told,

170

"We, who are many, are one body in Christ, and individually members one of another." When you think of an elbow, toe, knee, or ear standing by itself, it's evident that there is no strength there. In fact, severed from the rest of the body, those individual parts are most likely decaying. But joined to a healthy, thriving organism, they are useful, resilient, and fulfilling the roles they were created for.

So I believe it would be worthwhile to spend some time thinking about how our lives are stronger when we are meaningfully joined to the Body and have a reliable support system of brothers and sisters in Christ.

After all, no Christian has ever been called to "go it alone" in his or her walk of faith. We were created to exist in fellowship with and interdependence on one another. This is a concept that is essential for us to embrace if we want to stand strong, make a difference in this world, and impact eternity.

CALLED OUT TOGETHER

Of course, the idea of gathering together regularly with other believers is increasingly considered antiquated in today's world— especially with churches broadcasting their services on television or live-streaming them online. I can appreciate why people who are homebound or have no other options would find these very useful and uplifting.

But sadly, technology that was made to get the gospel outside the walls of the church or provide additional instruction has become a poor replacement for the Body of Christ for many who actually have local places of worship to attend. Somehow, in their minds, the weekly service has been reduced to some spiritual music and an encouraging message. Yet even in the earliest days of the church we see that "they were continually devoting themselves to the apostles' teaching and to fellowship, to the breaking of bread and to prayer" (Acts 2:42). There were very personal dimensions to church life. Believers took care of each other, helped each other grow in their faith, supported each other in times of need, and drew together as family. They were connected to each other as they matured in their walk with Christ.

Likewise, I hear people talking about the fact that they just don't *like* the church. I understand what they mean. Perhaps the preaching doesn't inspire or motivate them, the people are unkind, or there is something else in the style or administration that doesn't sit right with them. Many times, what people call "church" is more like a Christian club—organized for social purposes, to entertain, or to get some pet projects done.

Sadly, this just shows how far we have come from the church's original intent. The New Testament word for "church" is *ekklesia*, which means "called-out ones." We are called out of the world and assembled together to worship and serve the living God. So I am *not* talking about the church as a building made of bricks and mortar or merely a meeting place for Christians. Instead, it is you and I—a living, interconnected body made up of men and women indwelled by the Holy Spirit and called to accomplish God's awesome purposes on earth (Eph. 1:22–23).

When we think of this original meaning of the Body of Christ, it should actually be very convicting to us. Because if you are a Christian and claim you don't *like* the church, what you're really saying is that you do not like yourself. Because as a believer, you don't have a choice—by definition *you* are part of the Body of Christ.

Let me repeat that: *You are the church.*

You have been called out of the world and placed in an exclusive assembly that is prepared and empowered to glorify the living God. This is a membership that goes beyond style, polity, or organization. This is your new *family.* And you have a permanent part in it.

You not only have the privilege of using your gifts to help your brothers and sisters in the faith—you also have a responsibility to do so.

With that said, all of us have relatives we don't care much for, and there may be people in the church you don't particularly like. But as a member of the Body of Christ, you not only have the *privilege* of using your gifts to help your brothers and sisters in the faith grow in their relationships with Jesus—you also have a *responsibility* to do so.

DOING GREATER WORKS TOGETHER

Most of us know we are supposed to reach others with the gospel. We understand that we are called to faithfully teach the Word so that others can grow in their faith. But sometimes we are reluctant to pass on what we have been taught. Perhaps we are fearful we will fail or that doing so will require too much time, energy, and sacrifice. Possibly, we don't take the time to invest in others because we do not want to be hurt, we refuse to let them take the spotlight from us, or we're afraid they'll take advantage of us. It is so much easier to attend a meeting or to perform a task than to get involved in others' lives.

But we are called to have the same attitude as Jesus, who said, "I tell you the truth, anyone who believes in Me will do the same works I have done, and *even greater*

It is so much easier to attend a meeting or to perform a task than to get involved in others' lives.

works, because I am going to be with the Father" (John 14:12; emphasis added).

Can we *really* do greater work than Jesus? The Savior of the world? God Himself? We won't if we see our faith as solitary, individual, or unconnected. We won't if we see what we do in *comparison to* or in *competition with* others.

But if we see what we do as *building on the foundation He laid*, then yes, the works become greater and greater—exponentially so.

Therefore, we must also see that if we are truly serving Jesus— if His life is really flowing through us—those who follow us grow the influence and impact of our obedience to Him. This is the essence of Philippians 1:6: "He who began a good work in you will perfect it until the day of Christ Jesus." What you've done in faithful service to Jesus continues to bear spiritual fruit long after you are gone.

Ultimately, what God is doing is establishing an *eternal, unbroken line of relationships*. Just as other people told us about Jesus and helped us to grow in our faith, we are called to introduce others to Jesus, teaching them to follow Him and to reach others with the gospel. So even though the Father created us for Himself—to have an intimate relationship with Him—He also wants us to have eternal relationships with others. And it is through those connections and interactions that we actively live out what He is teaching us.

Think about what Jesus said in John 13:34–35: "A new commandment I give to you, that you love one another, even as I have loved you, that you also love one another. By this all men will know that you are My disciples, if you have love for one another."

Our love for one another is our mark of discipleship—the evidence that what Jesus has planted in us has taken root and is producing fruit. It is what shows others that there is power in a relationship with Christ, that there's something inherently different in those "called out," who have His life flowing through them. Of course, we are to show this love to everyone we meet—saved and unsaved alike. But what does it say about us when we refuse to engage in the one entity—the church—that Jesus told us we're part of and prayed we would be unified with (John 17:11)? I think it means we are missing out on a vital part of the life Christ has for us.

This is because the supernatural love of Jesus through the Body of Christ provides the fulfillment of the three essential things every person needs for a healthy self-image—what people require in order to feel that their lives have meaning and are worth living:

+ *A feeling of worthiness*—of being valuable

+ *A sense of belonging*—of being part of something important

+ *A recognition of competence*—of being capable

Think of this in terms of what we *receive* as part of the Body of Christ but also what we are called to *impart* to others.

First, people require a feeling of worthiness. We all need to know and believe that we are worth knowing and loving. Of course, we know that the most significant and costly sacrifice ever made was rendered for us. Jesus died on the cross because He loves us and wants an intimate relationship with us. He is the only One in all creation with the authority to assess our value, and in His wisdom, He made this appraisal: *You and I were worth dying for.* So as the Body of Christ, part of our responsibility is to remind each other of this important truth: that each of us has inestimable value because of the blood Jesus shed for us.

Do you believe this? You may say that you do, but is this truly how you treat every person you know? Do you look at each and every person you meet as someone God loves and sacrificed His Son to save? As Christ's representatives in this world, we must look at others through that lens. We must look at every person—regardless of wealth, education, social status, race, manners, or any other earthly measure—as someone Jesus loves enough to die for. And we should actively tell them the Good News of how profoundly loved they really are.

Second, people require a sense of belonging. We all need to feel as if we have a vital place as part of a group. And as we've just been discussing, you have been adopted into God's family forever. Galatians 4:4–5 says, "God sent forth His Son . . . so that He might redeem those who were under the Law, that we might receive the adoption as sons." In the Roman Empire, adoption was a very serious matter. Although parents could disown their natural children, an adopted child was in the family permanently, with rights and privileges to sonship that could never be taken away.

For us as believers, that means we have an extended family that includes all other believers in Jesus—past, present, and future, from all parts of the world, in heaven and on earth. You share a history and the blood of Jesus with them.

But more specifically, you have a role to play right where you are within a local body of believers, with Christians who live in your community and with whom you can worship, fellowship, serve, and seek God.

What is important for us to realize, however, is that within the Body of Christ there should be no outcasts. True, at times we must discipline (Matt. 18:15–17) and separate ourselves from other believers who cause divisions because of their heretical beliefs (2 John 1:7–11) or because they refuse to give up their ungodly behavior (1 Cor. 5).

But that isn't usually the reason we spurn other believers. Many times we reject others because we do not like their personality or they are unlike us in some way, such as politically or financially. We may have animosity toward them because of their nationality, background, economic status, race, or even because they simply do things differently from us. But we still have a responsibility to accept them as members of Christ's family just as Jesus did for us. As Paul wrote in Galatians 3:27–28, "All of you who were baptized into Christ have clothed yourselves with Christ. There is neither Jew nor Greek, there is neither slave nor free man, there is neither male nor female; for you are all one in Christ Jesus."

Jesus calls us to a high standard—to love others sacrificially as He did. In John 15:12–13, He said, "This is My commandment, that you love one another, just as I have loved you. Greater love has no one than this, that one lay down his life for his friends." So we see that not only are we to lay down our lives for fellow believers, but we must also put aside our opinions, rights, and goals to love others with the unconditional love that we have received from Christ. And yes, this includes those who've treated us badly (Luke 23:34; Eph. 4:32).

Finally, people require a recognition of competence. We all need to know that we're good at something, that we have a purpose that we can fulfill successfully. And as members of the Body of Christ, we all have an essential role in the church's well-being and effectiveness.

Not only are we to lay down our lives for fellow believers, but we must also put aside our opinions, rights, and goals to love others.

It seems, however, that some people accept this call and others don't. It has been widely noted that in most congregations, 80 percent of the work appears to be done by 20 percent of the people. This may give the impression that it is the normal dynamic of most organizations. But the church is the *Body* of Christ. So imagine if your physical body worked that way, with only 20 percent performing its functions. You would barely be able to get up from your sickbed.

Unfortunately, this is part of the problem with the church today, and a great deal of it is due to what we're teaching. After all, as we saw in the previous chapter, the Lord will enable us to do anything He calls us to do. But when we win people to Jesus, are we actively helping them find their part in the Body of Christ so they can use their gifts? Are we pouring our lives into others and showing them how to do so as well—so they can find their important part in God's eternal plan? And are we communicating how significant they are to the proper functioning of Jesus' Body on earth? Do we realize how crucial our participation is?

The point is that God created us with these needs so we would understand how essential He is to us, but also so we would recognize how profoundly we need one another. This is why no Christian has ever been called to "go it alone" in his or her walk of faith. The Christian life was meant to be lived out in relationships with other believers—both to live out our purposes and pass them on. So regardless of what we say we believe, what we truly think comes out in how we interact with others and how we respond to fellow members of the household of faith. This is yet another reason why so many believers feel weak but can't understand why: They simply aren't carrying out the purposes they were created for within the Body of Christ.

NECESSARY? REALLY?

Of course, many Christians think being involved in church isn't necessary because of the conflicts that occur between Christians. They tell themselves, *I don't think God has called me to put up with the complaining and bickering, the judging and the rejection. Surely, the Lord wants better for me than that!*

Yes, it is true that God doesn't want divisions and dissension in His Body (1 Cor. 1:10). He certainly does not want us to cause them. *But He never called us to avoid them either.* Instead, He calls us to be *peacemakers* of them—which both builds our character and strengthens the church (Matt. 5:9; 2 Tim. 2:14–16, 24–26). In fact, in Romans 12:18 we're instructed, "If possible, so far as it depends on you, be at peace with all men."

God's intention is for the parts of the Body of Christ to function together and be unified (John 17:22–23). Think about it: Why did Christ establish the church? Wasn't it to be His hands and feet in carrying out His mission? To give us guidance and direction for our lives; to provide strength, protection, and help in times of difficulty, which we all experience; and, of course, to be His representative to a lost and dying world?

And think about all He has called us to accomplish as His active agents on earth:

- *Evangelism*: Proclaiming the Good News of salvation through Jesus Christ (Mark 16:15; Acts 1:8).

- *Discipleship*: Teaching believers about their relationship with God, walking with them as they learn and grow, encouraging them to live in faith, and equipping them to serve Him. Jesus didn't call us to make converts. No, He called us to make disciples who know what He said and walk in His ways (Matt. 28:18–20).

- *Worship*: Creating opportunities for believers to focus exclusively on God—praising Him for His magnificent and eternal attributes, thanking Him for His love and provision, and experiencing His powerful presence (Ps. 95:6–7, 29:2).

- *Service*: Obeying what God calls us to do, supporting one another in our burdens, and reaching out to the lost in tangible ways to help them (Matt. 5:16; Gal. 6:2).

All this together is the wonderful work we're called to. But 20 percent of the congregation cannot do this for the entire church. Twenty percent of the Body cannot reach the world in the manner it was meant to. All of this requires us as believers to participate and have the life of Christ flowing through us. All of this requires unity.

That's why Hebrews 10:24–25 admonishes, "Let us consider how to stimulate one another to love and good deeds, not forsaking our own assembling together, as is the habit of some, but encouraging one another; and all the more as you see the day drawing near." Why? Because we *need* each other—not just to carry out the work of the church but also *to live the Christian life ourselves.* Our relationships with one another help us live out what God has called us to:

We are called to worship. When we gather as the church, we hear the testimonies of what God is doing in other people's lives—helping them, providing for them, delivering them from bondage—and it encourages us so that we can endure. Think about the songs you sing in church—how they remind you of the Father's truth and faithfulness. As we exalt Him together, we get a better picture of who He is and are able to remember who is defending and supplying us with what we need.

We are called to learn the Word of God. Likewise, we learn about God's Word from one another. There are things about Scripture that we may not know that others may have learned or gleaned from their research or time with the Father. Think about it: Why are you reading this book? If you didn't think that you could learn something new from God's Word or be invigorated in your struggle to stand strong, you wouldn't be reading it. But hopefully you have been encouraged, reminded of important principles, or learned something you can use in your life. Go to church with the same expectation—that there are things you can learn as the Holy Spirit speaks through the people in your congregations.

We are called to a support network. As the church, we are to love, build up, encourage, and serve one another. The church should be the place where we come to break free from our bondage, receive godly counsel, and find support to bear our burdens. We all face spiritual warfare and adversity. The church should be where we find refuge as we overcome it—to stand strong and endure until God provides the victory.

We are called to protect one another. Fellowshipping with other believers is meant to keep us from falling when the trials of life strike. When someone stops attending church and interacting with other Christians, it is almost inevitable that he or she will begin to drift away from God. This reminds me of a trip I took to Africa. We were going to photograph birds, but then I saw the lions in action—attacking a lone gazelle. It was fascinating. I learned that lions seldom attack the gazelle when it is in a herd. Instead, they find gazelles that are either along the edges of the pack or grazing by themselves. Then they can easily corner their prey and attack. Just as the gazelle is in danger when it is alone, so is the believer who stays on the fringes and does not become actively involved in the church. Alone, without spiritual support, encouragement, or instruction, that person becomes an easy target for the enemy, who prowls around like a roaring lion (1 Pet. 5:8). Think about it: If we aren't receiving counsel from godly believers, whom are we receiving it from? As believers, we keep each other accountable and encourage each other to stand firm in the faith, rather than fall into the traps of the enemy.

We are called to fulfill the Great Commission (Matt. 28:18–20). From the beginning, the reason Christianity spread is that each person took responsibility to tell others about the Good News of salvation through Jesus. We have to work together to do so, because we cannot reach the world on our own—just as the disciples couldn't. Together, we strengthen and broaden the church's impact on the world. You reach your fellow countrymen better than an outsider ever could. You know what challenges people in your community have and what ministry would have a great impact. As the Body of Christ, we can also work together to send missionaries around the world and support them through our prayers and financial support—as they take the Good News to the most remote places.

We are called to exercise spiritual gifts. The church is the best training ground for a person to discover, learn about, and develop his or her spiritual gifts and understand his or her purpose in God's overall plan. These gifts are in cooperation with one another—as we learn in 1 Corinthians 12:7 and 11: "To each one is given the manifestation of the Spirit for the common good . . . One and the same Spirit works all these things, distributing to each one individually just as He wills." The Holy Spirit is working out God's good purposes in the world and coordinating the Body to work together in achieving God's will. He knows where there is a need and what gift to give you in order to fill it. But the Holy Spirit does not work randomly. He has planned that you and I would discover and develop these gifts with other believers so we can use them wisely and effectively. Through other Christians, we have our questions answered, gain the courage to stretch into more challenging areas of ministry, receive comfort and understanding when we fail, and remain accountable. And we should do the same for others as well.

Now, I realize that this may be a far cry from what your church is actually doing. But as a vital member of Jesus' family, *you can make a difference.* You not only make your life stronger by serving, *you also make the Body of Christ healthier, more vital, and more robust by your input.* Galatians 6:9–10 admonishes, "Let us not lose heart in doing good, for in due time we will reap if we do not grow weary.

You not only make your life stronger by serving, you also make the Body of Christ healthier, more vital, and more robust by your input.

So then, while we have opportunity, let us do good to all people, and especially to those who are of the household of the faith."

In fact, if you have not seen the church fulfilling these roles, it is even more important that you engage. The family of God needs you—needs your gifts, strengths, talents, and testimony—to function, to endure, and to be reminded of its mission.

KEEP THE GOSPEL GOING

We might imagine the heaviness of Paul's heart as he sat in a Roman prison, awaiting his execution—the realization that soon the Roman government would take his life, and he would no longer be able to serve God on earth or minister to others. Certainly, he wanted all he had learned about Jesus and all he had done in obedience to the Savior to *endure*. But it seems that even more than that, his desire was for all believers to understand the incredibly important responsibility we've been given so that the gospel can continue beyond us as well.

We know this because it was during that time in prison that he wrote his second letter to Timothy, his son in the faith, and urged him, "You therefore, my son, be strong in the grace that is in Christ Jesus, and the things which you have heard from me in the presence of many witnesses, entrust these to faithful men who will be able to teach others also" (2 Tim. 2:1–2).

Paul exhorts Timothy to keep on preaching the gospel faithfully despite the challenges because the message of salvation is so eternally important. But Paul also reminds Timothy of how crucial it is that he convey what he has learned to those who will likewise pass on what they've received.

You see, a danger exists for us as believers. We can get caught up in thinking that it is all about us—*our* achievements, *our* relationship with God, *our* trials, and what *we* are learning. But we actually experience these things in order to benefit those who come after us (2 Cor. 1:3–7, 4:11–12).

When Paul says, "Be strong in the grace that is in Christ Jesus" (2 Tim. 2:1), it is because he acknowledges there will be challenges and that it will be necessary for us to embrace God's grace as we do what He has called us to do. That grace and power are available *in* us, first, and then *through* us, second—*in us* as we endure the trials that arise and *through us* as we equip others in the Body of Christ. It is a constant flow—from God to us and then to others. If we do not allow that grace to have an outlet, we stagnate.

> *We get caught up in thinking that it is all about us—our achievements, our relationship with God, our trials, and what we are learning. But we actually experience these things in order to benefit those who come after us.*

We can actually see an illustration of this in the geography of Israel. The Sea of Galilee is beautiful and teeming with life. There are still all kinds of fish there—tilapia, carp, and sardines to name a few. On the other hand, the Dead

Sea is just that—dead. It smells terrible. Although there are many minerals there, it doesn't sustain life.

What is the difference between the two? The Sea of Galilee has an outlet. The Jordan River flows into it from the north and out of it from the south. But the Dead Sea has no outlet. The Jordan River flows in, but nothing flows out. Instead, the minerals gather there, choking out the very life they were created to sustain.

Some believers seem to know a lot about Scripture, theology, and doctrine, but they are as mean as snakes. The grace and power of God stagnates within them. Day after day, week after week, year after year they receive the truth of God's Word, but they never live it out or pass on to others the wonderful principles they have learned.

In fact, they may even be active in the church, sitting on committees or attending meetings. But are they actively getting involved in other people's lives? Are they living out the wonderful spiritual gifts the Holy Spirit has given them "for the common good" (1 Cor. 12:7)? No. They don't embrace who they are or the purpose for which God created them. They do not allow the life of Christ to flow through them to others. They aren't entrusting what the Father has shown them to faithful believers "who will be able to teach others also" (2 Tim. 2:2).

Some fail to let God's grace and power flow through them because they believe they need to be better equipped. They are afraid they don't know enough or that others are more skilled than they are. So they put it off, always thinking they will have time later to make disciples as Jesus commanded. But we must never underestimate how much we have to teach others.

In Romans 13, Paul writes, "Owe nothing to anyone except to love one another; for he who loves his neighbor has fulfilled the law . . . Do this, knowing the time, that it is already the hour for you to awaken from sleep; for now salvation is nearer to us than when we believed. The night is almost gone, and the day is near" (vv. 8, 11–12). In other words, our responsibility is to lovingly guide others in their relationship with Christ because the time for us to see Jesus face-to-face draws ever closer.

We must never underestimate how much we have to teach others.

The truth of the matter is that we do not know when our time will come. All of us have known people who died suddenly, without any warning. One moment they are making all kinds of plans for the future, and the next they are "absent from the body and . . . at home with the Lord" (2 Cor. 5:8). Likewise, no one knows the day or the hour when Jesus is coming back (Matt. 24:36). So it is extremely important for us to make the most of every opportunity (Col. 4:2–6).

FINDING YOUR TIMOTHIES

Paul poured his life and ministry into Timothy, and he encouraged Timothy to do the same. As a result, God worked through what the apostle Paul did in an incredible way.

So my challenge to you today is that you pray about who the Father has for you to raise up as a Timothy. Once He shows you whom it is you are to pour your life into, set about training that person, with the idea of inspiring him or her to raise up his or her own Timothies.

How do we do this? How do we know who needs our time and direction? As in everything else, we must pray and seek God's choice for us.

We saw this when the Lord chose David to be the king of Israel. If you recall, He sent the prophet Samuel to Bethlehem to speak with Jesse about anointing one of his sons as the next king.

> Samuel replied, "I have come to sacrifice to the Lord. Purify yourselves and come with me to the sacrifice." Then Samuel performed the purification rite for Jesse and his sons and invited them to the sacrifice, too.
>
> When they arrived, Samuel took one look at Eliab and thought, "Surely this is the Lord's anointed!"
>
> But the Lord said to Samuel, "Don't judge by his appearance or height, for I have rejected him. The Lord doesn't see things the way you see them. People judge by outward appearance, but the Lord looks at the heart." (1 Sam. 16:5–7 NLT)

You may know the rest of the story. Seven of Jesse's sons passed before Samuel, and none of them was chosen. The boy God wanted was the one who was out tending the sheep, not even worthy to be called in to participate in the sacrifice with the rest.

Why did the Lord choose David? Because he was a man after God's heart (Acts 13:22). Because as the world watched the outward appearance of those brothers, the Lord watched as they worshipped Him and served Him. And He saw that David was the only one with the potential to submit to Him as the king of Israel would be required to.

Therefore, we have to let God lead us before we can lead others. The Lord showed Samuel whom to choose, and He will faithfully confirm His will to us as well. We must allow the Father to reveal whom to invest in, because He knows not only who is worthy of our efforts but also whom we are equipped to lead successfully.

Jesus gives us a great pattern to follow. Do you recall how He chose the apostles? Luke 6:12–13 tells us Jesus "went off to the mountain to pray, and He spent the whole night in prayer to God. And when day came, He called His disciples to Him and chose twelve of them, whom He also named as apostles."

We may think that Jesus was walking along one day and He just started choosing people. But the truth is that He had known them and walked with them for some time already. Notice that Christ called all of His disciples to Himself, and out of the group He chose twelve of them. And before He chose the twelve, He spent the whole night in prayer to God.

So that is the pattern. You walk with people, observe them, and pray to God about them. And as the Father reveals whom to invest in, you obey Him.

A TIME OF REFLECTION

Friend, I know it may sound counterintuitive to pour your life into others, especially when you are facing your own storms of life. But remember, Paul never had an easy time of it. In 2 Corinthians 11:23–28 he recounts his numerous sufferings:

Imprisonments, beaten times without number, often in danger of death. Five times I received from the Jews thirty-nine lashes. Three times I was beaten with rods, once I was stoned, three times I was shipwrecked, a night and a day I have spent in the deep. I have been on frequent journeys, in dangers from rivers, dangers from robbers, dangers from my countrymen, dangers from the Gentiles, dangers in the city, dangers in the wilderness, dangers on the sea, dangers among false brethren; I have been in labor and hardship, through many sleepless nights, in hunger and thirst, often without food, in cold and exposure. Apart from such external things, there is the daily pressure on me of concern for all the churches.

Yes, Paul faced many devastating hardships and trials. Yet Paul testified about what gave him joy:

Therefore if there is any encouragement in Christ, if there is any consolation of love, if there is any fellowship of the Spirit, if any affection and compassion, *make my joy complete by being of the same mind, maintaining the same love, united in spirit, intent on one purpose.* Do nothing from selfishness or empty conceit, but with humility of mind regard one another as more important than yourselves; *do not merely look out for your own personal interests, but also for the interests of others.* (Phil. 2:1–4; emphasis added)

In other words, his joy came from allowing the life of Christ to flow through him to others. His fulfillment came in seeing people rightly related to the Lord and serving God faithfully. It encouraged Paul to see Jesus glorified through the people he'd ministered to.

This is because a strong life isn't just about what happens to you; it's also about whom you have around you and how you're strengthening them. When you see God working powerfully through someone you've invested in, there is an indescribable fulfillment and joy that fills you to the very core of who you are. Through it the Father gives you strength that helps you endure just as He did for Paul, and brings forth fruit from your life that lasts into eternity.

A strong life isn't just about what happens to you; it's also about whom you have around you and how you're strengthening them.

So for the next few minutes, I challenge you to pray—asking God for His direction and guidance about your part in the Body of Christ. Use the prayer below, and ask the Father to lead you in the following areas, then write down whatever He brings to mind.

Father, I want to live a strong life, and I accept that this means I must be a willing and active participant in the Body of Christ. Am I—as Your servant—all You desire me to be? Am I serving in the way You created me to and carrying out the good works You planned for me to accomplish?

Father, in what areas am I failing You by neglecting the gifts You have given me to share? Am I doing all that You desire for me to do—in Your power and to Your glory?

Father, is there anyone I need to forgive—in my church, community, or other ministries?

Father, is there anyone in my congregation or community

that I am neglecting? People I should be serving or recruiting for service?

Father, is there anyone You wish me to mentor? Please show me who my Timothies are. Show me whom You wish me to raise up as my spiritual children.

Father, is there anything I need to let go of and entrust to another person?

Father, is there any new ministry area You desire me to pursue or people You desire to reach through me?

Father, where am I wasting time on activities or pursuits that are not eternal? What tasks do I need to eliminate in order to serve You as wisely as possible and be a good steward of what You have given me?

Father, my life belongs to You. My heart, soul, mind, and strength are Yours. Help me to love others sacrificially as You would. Give me spiritual eyes to see the spiritual gifts others have, the wounds they carry, and how You desire me to encourage them.

Continue to teach me Your truth through Your Word so that others may believe, be saved, break free from the bondage to sin, and find their place in the Body of Christ.

Bring spiritual awakening to my community, revival to Your church, and unity between all the brothers and sisters in Christ. I pray that You would be glorified among us in a greater way than we have ever seen before and that our Savior Jesus would be exalted in the hearts and lives of everyone I meet.

May Your life flow through us in powerful and wonderful ways we've never imagined. Thank You, Lord, for strengthening me and strengthening others through the work You are doing in me.

In the matchless name of Jesus I pray. Amen.

9

YOUR CONVICTIONS ABOUT ADVERSITY

Burden or Bridge?

*P*erhaps you noticed in the last chapter that we discussed how you are to view your interaction with others without much mention of how you have been treated. This may strike you as strange, especially if you are in the throes of a difficult spiritual battle and are seeking to stand strong. Maybe you are experiencing painful indifference from people you love or from people who are supposed to love you. It could be that others have been cruel or unjust toward you. Or you may be struggling with any number of issues that make you feel utterly isolated and alone and you wonder why there isn't anyone who will share this burden with you. So the fact that we have been addressing only *your* role in standing strong may be disconcerting to you.

But this has been because no matter what your adversity may be or what source it comes from, *what truly matters is your attitude toward it*. What you believe. How you respond. How you take action. Where you ultimately find your comfort and strength.

Because that is what really determines whether or not you will stand strong.

The truth of the matter is, you and I will face difficulties as long as we've breath in our lungs. This is for several reasons, of course.

First, as a believer, you will likely draw adversity if you are faithful to the Lord God. Your life, beliefs, morals, and even your presence will be convicting and confusing to those who do not know Christ as Savior, making them uncomfortable. Some will accept Jesus' offer of salvation because of His work through you, but others will lash out, opposing you and refusing to believe in the gracious gift of the Savior (John 17:14–15).

Second, you will face challenges because the strong life is based on your utter dependence on God, and that means He will allow situations to arise that stretch your faith in Him and your love for others (Isa. 30:20–21).

Third, you will experience adversity because we live in a fallen world, where people can be difficult and life can be unpredictable. So if you are going to help people to become who God created them to be—as we discussed in the last chapter—it is helpful for you to understand the struggles they're facing. You may have different cultures, disagree politically, or have dissimilar tastes, but the one place of common ground you can usually find with others is in the suffering you've experienced. Everyone knows what it means to hurt, fear for the future, and need hope. So the Father works through your brokenness, failings, needs, and trials to help others and lead them to Jesus (2 Cor. 1:3–7).

IT'S ABOUT *HOW* YOU DEAL WITH IT

As I just said, the key to adversity is *how it is handled*—whether you think of it as a burden that weighs you down and destroys you, or whether you humble yourself before the Father and allow Him to teach and mold you through it.

This is why it is so important to seek God's wisdom about whatever adversity we face. If we interpret the trials that occur in our lives with our limited understanding, it will certainly depress and discourage us. We will try to dull the pain with alcohol, drugs, sex, gambling, or some other destructive behavior. Again, as we saw in Proverbs 14:12 and 16:25, this is because "there is a way which seems right to a man, but its end is the way of death." Our interpretation of what is happening to us is faulty, which means our manner of dealing with it will be flawed as well.

But if we "lean not on our own understanding" (Prov. 3:5–6) and trust God, He will show us the "path of life" (Ps. 16:11) through everything we experience.

This is because the problems you face are not a mistake or random. Likewise, you should never think that they are evidence of God punishing you or being cruel to you (Heb. 12:5–11). In fact, Lamentations 3:33 reminds us, "He does not willingly bring affliction or grief to anyone" (NIV).

Rather, the adversity you are enduring has been *allowed*—not necessarily *caused* by the Lord but *permitted* by Him in His wisdom—and *will* benefit you in some way. This is the wonderful truth we see in Romans 8:28: "We know that God causes all things to work together for good to those who love God, to those who are called according to His purpose." The Father works *every single detail* to your advantage.

As George Müller famously said, "In a thousand trials, it is not just five hundred of them that work 'for the good' of the believer, but nine hundred and ninety-nine, plus one."

So from God's perspective, adversity is the path to freedom, healing, establishing, and strengthening you (1 Pet. 5:10). He uses difficulties to liberate you of whatever is hindering Christ's life from flowing through you. Paul expressed this truth in 2 Corinthians 1:8–9:

> *The Father works* every single detail *to your advantage.*

"We do not want you to be unaware, brethren, of our affliction which came to us in Asia, that we were burdened excessively, beyond our strength, so that we despaired even of life; indeed, we had the sentence of death within ourselves so that we would not trust in ourselves, but in God who raises the dead."

Even the great apostle Paul faced terrible trials that were beyond his power to endure. Yet he saw the value in them—they were teaching him not to trust in himself but to rely fully on God and His ability to bestow the resurrection-life on us.

This is why I've placed adversity in the "build with" portion of this book. Because what is God's ultimate goal for us? Romans 8:29 tells us, "Those whom He foreknew, He also predestined to become conformed to the image of His Son." Therefore, through difficulties, He is establishing the eternal, irreplaceable, mighty likeness of Christ in us in many ways—ways that help us endure and "overwhelmingly conquer" in the storms of life (Rom. 8:27). So let's look at what God is trying to form in us as He establishes the likeness of Christ in us.

The likeness of Christ's freedom.

Our Savior was completely sinless. Although He shared in our humanity in every way, He was never under the control of sin.

But this bondage to sin is something the rest of us struggle with, and it makes us very weak. It will never separate us eternally from the Lord again after salvation, but it does hinder our relationship with Him and our ability to enjoy all God has for us—including His resurrection power. Paul expressed this in Romans 7:22–25: "I love God's law with all my heart. But there is another power within me that is at war with my mind. This power makes me a slave to the sin that is still within me. Oh, what a miserable person I am! Who will free me from this life that is dominated by sin and death? Thank God! The answer is in Jesus Christ our Lord."

Through adversity, the Holy Spirit is actively and continually setting us free from that enslavement to sin and giving us the victory in Jesus. The Lord forces those areas of sinfulness to the surface and helps us to obey Him, breaking through the chains that hold us captive.

The likeness of Christ's character.

Of course, through adversity God also builds Christ's character in us. He desires to mold us so that our personhood reflects Jesus: We think the way He thinks, love the way He loves, forgive the way He forgives, and see people as He sees them. Likewise, "love, joy, peace, patience, kindness, goodness, faithfulness, gentleness, [and] self-control" become the natural outflow of

Through adversity, the Holy Spirit is actively and continually setting us free from enslavement to sin.

197

our lives (Gal. 5:22–23). As we said previously, we cannot produce these character traits on a consistent basis in our own strength.

So, through adversity, God teaches us the importance of integrity, honesty, humility, compassion, kindness, holiness, and grace. We see that sin is just not worth its consequences. For example, once you get caught in a lie, you realize it isn't worth it to stray from the truth. But also, as we are freed from the sinful ways we provide for our own needs, we will begin to be more godly and act more like Christ.

The likeness of Christ's confidence.

Through difficulties, the Father builds our reliance on Him. Think about it: Did Jesus ever doubt God? Of course not! Likewise, hardships are afforded to us for the purpose of sifting out all our uncertainties and misgivings about the Father. As 1 Peter 1:6–7 reminds us, "In this you greatly rejoice, even though now for a little while, if necessary, you have been distressed by various trials, so that the proof of your faith, being more precious than gold which is perishable, even though tested by fire, may be found to result in praise and glory and honor at the revelation of Jesus Christ." In other words, through trials, your faith or confidence in God is made sure. You are forced to stop relying on anything but the Lord.

The likeness of Christ's obedience.

Hebrews 5:8 testifies, "Although [Jesus] was a Son, He learned obedience from the things which He suffered." Even though Jesus is God in the flesh, *it took an act of His will to obey when pain and affliction were involved.* This is because anyone can submit to another's authority when there are rewards promised—when there is joy and ease ahead. But when the immediate effect of our obedience is hardship, the decision is not so easy.

Adversity makes us decide whether we really believe in the Lord and respect Him as God by obeying Him.

We saw Jesus make this decision at Gethsemane, when He said, "Father, if You are willing, remove this cup from Me; yet not My will, but Yours be done" (Luke 22:42).

Likewise, when we choose the difficult path—even when we don't understand what the Father is doing or simply cannot imagine how the Lord could work things out for our good—it cements our commitment to Him. Obeying God in the tough decisions readies us for both His assignments and His great blessings.

The likeness of Christ's heart.

Once you've suffered greatly, you're much less likely to judge others for their trials. However, adversity also makes us much better servants of God because it deepens our ability to minister to others. We have a much more profound perspective on what questions and hurts plague the hearts of others and how to comfort, encourage, and counsel them.

This is why 2 Corinthians 1:3–4 teaches, "Blessed be the God and Father of our Lord Jesus Christ, the Father of mercies and God of all comfort, who comforts us in all our affliction so that we will be able to comfort those who are in any affliction with the comfort with which we ourselves are comforted by God." The Lord gives meaning to our pain when we can turn it around and use it to help others in their time of need.

The likeness of Christ's focus.

Where did Jesus always go whenever He was about to make a decision or take an important step? To the Father. Jesus never relied on earthly sources of counsel, provision, or power. He never sought other men's approval. His complete focus was on God at all times.

This is what adversity teaches us as well. Earthly sources of guidance, security, and comfort always fail. But the Lord Almighty *never* fails! So God actively gets our focus off them and onto Himself. And we're reminded that our "momentary, light affliction is producing for us an eternal weight of glory far beyond all comparison, while we look not at the things which are seen, but at the things which are not seen; for the things which are seen are temporal, but the things which are not seen are eternal" (2 Cor. 4:17–18). In other words, we keep what really matters—the eternal—in view.

The likeness of Christ's mission.

Because God is building His eternal perspective in us, we begin to realize that our relationships with others and our objective in regard to them must also change. No longer can we deem people as acceptable or unworthy by earthly standards, but must see them as souls trapped in sin and driven by its destructive power. For believers caught in their transgressions, we grieve that they are not experiencing the freedom Jesus died to give them (Rom. 6; Gal. 5:1). For the lost, their blindness at His gift and future demise in hell makes us weep as it made Christ weep (Luke 19:41). So adversity helps us to take on Jesus' mission—not to be served but to serve and to give our lives freely so others can be saved and experience all He has for them (Matt. 20:28).

God is establishing the likeness of Christ's power.

Finally, adversity helps us experience Christ's resurrection power. Remember, there is no resurrection without our first experiencing a death. This is why Paul said,

> "I count all things to be loss in view of the surpassing value of knowing Christ Jesus my Lord, for whom I have suffered the loss of all things, and count them but rubbish so that I may gain Christ . . . that I may know [Christ] and the power of His resurrection and the fellowship of His sufferings, *being conformed to His death; in order that I may attain to the resurrection from the dead.*" (Phil. 3:8, 10–11; emphasis added)

As we've talked about before, there must be an end to our self-reliance, so we can rely solely on God and His power can flow through us.

I heard an interesting illustration of this from a plumber. He said that when repairing a system, he must wait until the pipes are completely dry before he can work on them. If there is even a drop of water left in the system, there is absolutely no point in trying to fix it. This is because if there is any moisture, the heat from the soldering torch goes into turning the water to steam rather than repairing the system.

As long as there is even a drop of self-reliance in us, we will fight God from healing us and working through us.

This is a striking picture of the Christian life. As long as there is even a drop of self-reliance in us, we will fight God from healing us and working through us—from allowing His life to course through us. And so, through difficulties and challenges, the Lord cleans all that out so that we will be effective conduits for His resurrection power.

READIED TO RESPOND

Of course, if you've spent any time in church, you may already know many of the benefits of adversity. You may understand mentally that God disciplines you for your good. Yet problems can still blindside you and knock you off balance, can't they? They can still shake you to the core, making you question all you believe. This is particularly true when you are a believer trying to honor the Lord. The disconnect between your intellectual understanding of God's character and the genuine pain of your emotions can seem as far as the east is from the west. How does one allow for the other? How can the two possibly coexist?

So, when we experience this seeming disconnect, a natural question arises: *What is real? What do I really have to rely on and respond to?* After all, you can't see or touch the Father; yet your struggle is not only tangible—it's clobbering you in very profound ways.

Perhaps the difficulty comes through the circumstances you're experiencing—financial, physical, or relational setbacks that seem to contradict a promise He's made you. It could be that the doctor tells you that a loved one will always be in pain or has a short time to live.

Or maybe you are facing opposition from others who are

supposed to be on your side. You have loved them, helped them, and served them faithfully, but they still act hatefully toward you.

It could even be that you sought God's guidance in an important situation. You wrestled with trying to understand what He wanted you to do and obeyed Him as well as you knew how. And you still failed.

The battle between your heart and head can become very confusing indeed, because it feels so personal. You may ask, "Why would a good and loving God allow me to suffer in this manner, especially when I am doing my best for Him?"

And of course in the middle of it all is our enemy, who is constantly feeding us messages that separate us from God. He tells us that the Father does not love us. That the Savior has abandoned us. That the Lord will never come through for us. He is *able* to help, but we are so defective that He refuses to intervene on our behalf. All of this is meant to tempt us to fulfill our needs in our own way and in our own strength—in other words, to bypass what God is doing in and through us by taking control.

But we must remember that adversity is the process by which we grow spiritually—and it is progressive, continually requiring the stretching of our faith (Rom. 1:17). At salvation we are born again—we are given life spiritually. And we must truly view it as a holy conception: What was *not in existence* or living (our spirit) is *now alive* and growing.

Just as a newborn baby has a limited aptitude to take in his or her surroundings, we also have a limited capacity for knowing and understanding God. But just as that child needs to grow in an abundance of ways so do we.

Think about a baby who is developing. How does that sweet

child learn? By *doing*, naturally. Children learn to talk by making sounds. Eventually they realize that certain sounds represent specific concepts. In due time, they learn to put the words together to establish thoughts.

All along the way they are stretching their limits and, as parents, we help our children to do so. We help them sound things out. We hold up objects and tell them the words associated with them. By repetition we help them understand the world around them and how to express themselves in it. In due course, as their capacity for language increases, we teach them to speak in sentences and read—helping them to comprehend not only concrete concepts such as Daddy or bowl but also abstract ideas such as right and wrong.

Well, that is why God allows adversity into our lives—He is stretching our limits to grow us. The difference is that the Father is not broadening us physically or mentally; He's augmenting our *spiritual* capability. Why? Because the life the Lord has for us is increasingly revealed to us—from faith to faith—as our ability to receive Him is expanded. As our good and faithful Father, He teaches us to walk with Him through His wisdom and care.

The life the Lord has for us is increasingly revealed as our ability to receive Him is expanded.

However, whether or not you grow is somewhat dependent upon how you respond to Him when adversity strikes. This is why you will see some believers maturing by leaps and bounds, while others have known Christ for years and are still mired in their earthly ways. The former use the troubles they experience as a bridge to a deeper relationship with Christ, while the latter see difficulties as burdens they cannot overcome and reasons for distrusting the Father. Please allow me to explain.

BURDEN OR BRIDGE?

When troubles arise, if you choose to respond to them in your own strength, with your own resources, you will invariably see them as *burdens*—especially the bigger and more difficult they are. The evidence that this is how you are responding is that you

+ *blame God.* You think of Him as cruel or uncaring and become bitter toward Him because He allowed the problem to plague you.

+ *try to escape.* You may turn to something other than the Father to alleviate your pain—drugs, alcohol, sex, gluttony, or some other sin.

+ *feel sorry for yourself.* You see yourself as a victim.

+ *fail in your faith.* You trust your doubts about God more than God Himself and turn to your own means for solving your problems.

+ *walk away from God altogether.* You turn away from God as the source of your comfort and guidance, and decide that the Christian life just isn't worth the sacrifice.

Sadly, if you choose to respond to adversity as a burden, it becomes a roadblock to your spiritual growth. First, it drives you away from the Father because you devote all your strength, intellect, and emotions to overcoming your problem rather than turning to Him. In a sense, that problem becomes your god because it consumes your focus.

Likewise, you no longer trust the Lord because He didn't stop the storms from happening. This, of course, creates emotional bondage—bitterness, jealousy, resentment, despair, and discouragement—because you feel helpless and purposeless. You are cut off from the One who is able to deliver you and who gives your life meaning and joy.

Then, as you struggle with all of these destructive emotions, it affects your relationships. You are bitter, unforgiving, and self-focused, making it difficult for you to be kind, generous, and constructive toward others.

Finally, treating your struggles as burdens can even damage your health. Stress and anxiety have been proved to cause everything from heart and respiratory problems to cancer and autoimmune diseases.

Is this what you desire? Bitterness? Broken relationships? Damaged health? Alienation from the Father? Of course not.

Thankfully, God gives us another way, which is to see trials as a *bridge* to a more profound relationship with Him. In fact, adversity is the Father's most effective tool for deepening our faith and commitment to Him and for carrying out His purposes in our lives. Suffering is the setback from which we can take our greatest spiritual leaps forward.

Of course, this takes a dynamic change in our mind-set about the Lord. This entails a dramatic stretching of our faith. This requires us to acknowledge that as children of our sovereign God, we are never victims of our circumstances. This forces us to choose to believe Him over what we see and feel and hear—for us to answer the question, *What is real?* with, "Let God be found true!" (Rom. 3:4).

This is the essence of Proverbs 3:5–6: "Trust in the Lord with all your heart and do not lean on your own understanding. In all your ways acknowledge Him, and He will make your paths straight."

Leaning on your own understanding means relying on your senses and mental capabilities. You assess your situation from your human standpoint and act accordingly. And God says, "Don't do that."

Instead, faith acknowledges the Lord's perspective and trusts His sovereign care over every detail of our lives. It asserts, "Reality is what God says it is!"

This is why Scripture becomes our anchor in times of storm. We say, "Yes, this is beyond my control. But my Savior has proved Himself all-powerful, all-knowing, and unconditionally loving throughout history. He lives in me, and I trust Him to make something good out of everything I face." When you do this, your spiritual growth takes off. Your capacity to know and trust God increases exponentially. And as we saw at the beginning of this chapter, the result is

> *Faith acknowledges the Lord's perspective and trusts His sovereign care over every detail of our lives.*

+ a deeper relationship with God

+ freedom from sin

+ an increasingly Christ-like character

- ✦ a strengthened faith

- ✦ preparation for God's purposes

- ✦ a greater understanding of ourselves

- ✦ increasing effectiveness for God

- ✦ the ability to help others through their adversity

So the way to overcome any challenge is to always remember God's involvement in our lives.

JOSEPH'S EXAMPLE

One of the great examples in Scripture of a man who was made strong through adversity by trusting God is Joseph. Most likely, you know this story, but it is worth thinking about in terms of seeing your adversity as a bridge.

If you recall, Joseph was born into a troubled family, where his father Jacob had two wives who were constantly competing for his affection and attention. This ultimately resulted in the births of thirteen children—twelve boys and one girl (Gen. 29:15–30:24, 35:18).

From early on, Joseph stood out from among his numerous siblings as his father's favorite. Likewise, the Lord blessed Joseph with dreams that indicated he had a prestigious and fruitful future ahead. In fact, Joseph's visions foreshadowed that he would become a great and mighty ruler and even his family would bow to him (Gen. 37:3–8). Joseph responded in faith *despite* his many adversities:

Despite rejection.

Unfortunately, Joseph's dreams and his interpretations of them caused his brothers to despise him so deeply that they "plotted against him to put him to death" (Gen. 37:18). Ultimately, the brothers threw him in a pit. When some Ishmaelite merchants came by, the brothers pulled Joseph out of the pit and sold him to them for twenty shekels of silver (Gen. 37:28). These merchants took him to Egypt, where he was purchased by Potiphar, the captain of Pharaoh's royal guard (Gen. 39:1).

We now know that this was the Lord moving Joseph to the nation where he would one day rule in God's time—Egypt. But Joseph certainly could not see that from his point of view. Rather, from where he was, he'd been rejected by his own family and his situation was absolutely disheartening. He went from being his father's favorite and a free man in a wealthy family with a promising future to a penniless slave in a foreign country where he had no rights or privileges. We could certainly understand if Joseph had chosen to give up hope at this point, as most of us would.

But instead of becoming bitter, focusing on the actions of his brothers, or taking on the attitude of a victim, Joseph continued to have faith in the Lord, bravely making the best of his circumstances.

In other words, Joseph didn't lean on *his* understanding of the situation; rather, *he honored God by working hard.* Genesis 39:2–3 testifies, "The Lord was with Joseph, so he became a successful man . . . His master saw that the Lord was with him and how the Lord caused all that he did to prosper in his hand." In this way, Joseph remained in the center of God's will and eventually won Potiphar's favor.

Despite injustice.

Now, as you may know, Joseph's success in Potiphar's household was short-lived. Potiphar's wife saw that Joseph was a handsome young man and attempted to seduce him. He rejected her advances, saying, "My master trusts me with everything in his entire household. No one here has more authority than I do. He has held back nothing from me except you, because you are his wife. How could I do such a wicked thing? It would be a great sin against God" (Gen. 39:8–9 NLT). Joseph did what was right and again honored the Lord.

At this point, in our human estimation, there should have been a celebration for Joseph, seeing that he had acted so admirably. We would imagine that a great reward awaited his unyielding faithfulness. Instead, however, Potiphar's wife was infuriated that Joseph had refused her, so she framed him and had him sent to jail (Gen. 39:20).

Again, Joseph could have gotten angry at the Lord and blamed Him for all his misfortunes. That would have been the normal human response. From his point of view, his situation went from bad to worse—he'd gone from a free man to a slave to a prisoner, even though he had remained faithful and had done nothing wrong. It wasn't right—especially for one dedicated to God.

Perhaps you know how this feels. You've trusted in the wise and omnipotent hand of the Father and have honored Him, but it seemed that when you needed Him most He *appeared* to be noticeably absent from your circumstances. You were maligned, though you had done nothing wrong. You were unjustly treated, though you were representing Christ. I say He *appeared* to be absent because He was undoubtedly still there, guiding you, though you could not see Him.

This was certainly true for Joseph.

Because we know the story, we understand that, first, the Lord was positioning Joseph to meet the chief cupbearer, who would eventually introduce Joseph to Pharaoh at the precise moment when he was needed most. But Joseph didn't know that.

Second, we know that God continually increased Joseph's responsibilities in order to train him to lead. He went from overseeing Potiphar's large household to the even greater task of managing all of the prisoners. Genesis 39:22–23 tells us, "The chief jailer committed to Joseph's charge all the prisoners who were in the jail; so that whatever was done there, he was responsible for it. The chief jailer did not supervise anything under Joseph's charge because the Lord was with him; and whatever he did, the Lord made to prosper."

Again, this may not have been obvious from Joseph's perspective until much later. But we see that God was indeed active in Joseph's situation, and we see the incredible wisdom Joseph showed when he chose not to become bitter but instead decided to become better.

Despite the wait.

We know that in God's time, Joseph's dreams came true. It took years, of course—*thirteen* years, to be precise. But eventually Joseph met Pharaoh and was the Lord's chosen instrument to save not only Egypt—and indeed people throughout the earth, from seven years of famine—but his family as well (Gen. 41).

But none of that was obvious until it happened. In the middle of the storm, things always look terrible.

Just think about all Joseph faced: hatred and rejection by his family, the helplessness of being sold into slavery, the injustice of being wrongly accused when he was simply honoring God and the authority over him, and the humiliation of being thrown into jail indefinitely without cause.

Imagine all those years of not knowing what was going on, seeing only defeat after defeat, heartbreak after heartbreak.

Any of us could have become resentful after all of that. Any of us could have given up hope. The point is that for thirteen years, Joseph endured through increasingly worsening conditions until God raised him up to be one of the most important figures in Jewish history.

We know the end of his story. But we don't know the end of our own stories. And that's what makes it so hard for us to trust when we face rejection, hatred, helplessness, injustice, wrongful accusations, humiliation, defeat after defeat, heartbreak after heartbreak, and countless years of waiting to see the Lord's deliverance. Any of us can become bitter after all of that if we see our adversity as a burden.

Imagine what the Father could do through you if you would exhibit the same quality of faith that we see in Joseph.

But God knows the end of your story, just as He knew how and where He was leading Joseph. And His desire is that, like Joseph, you will see it all as a bridge to a deeper relationship with Him.

Even though he did not understand it all, Joseph continued to have faith that the Lord was in control. He was confident that God was sovereign over everything that touched his life—including the adversity. How do we know this? From his testimony in Genesis 50:20: "You meant evil against me, but God meant it for good in order to bring about this present result, to preserve many people alive."

Imagine what the Father could do through you if you would exhibit the same quality of faith.

TRIUMPH AHEAD

You are always wise when you remember God's greater purposes in whatever you're going through. This is why we are told, "The fear of the Lord is the beginning of wisdom, and the knowledge of the Holy One is understanding" (Prov. 9:10).

So how can you stand strong through your troubles like Joseph did? It's what we have been discussing throughout this book.

First, start with God's Word and decide beforehand that you're going to honor the Lord, regardless of what happens or what He asks of you.

You cannot wait until you're in the midst of trouble to get into Scripture or to choose to obey God. Because when adversity strikes, you are more likely to be confused or react in your flesh rather than respond in a way that honors the Lord.

As we saw at the very beginning of this book, Jesus said, "Everyone who hears these words of Mine and acts on them, may be compared to a wise man who built his house on the rock" (Matt. 7:24). The only basis for a rock-solid foundation is God's Word. So be the kind of person who regularly reads, meditates on, and obeys Scripture—accepting His truth and putting the principles of His

Word into practice. Lay the foundation of a strong faith and life by allowing the Lord to guide your thinking. This will help keep you strong and in the center of His will. And if the Father identifies something in your life that displeases Him, make sure you repent of it as soon as you are aware of it so that it will not become a foothold for the enemy.

Second, make sure your main focus is God Himself.

When troubles are lined up against you, don't measure them against your limited power, wisdom, and resources. Instead, think about them in terms of what the Lord can do. He is the omnipotent, omniscient, and omnipresent Creator of all that exists, who loves you unconditionally. Is anything too difficult for Him? Absolutely not.

Rather, remember that God's main goal for your life is intimacy with Himself. He wants you to get your eyes off yourself and *know Him.* And so He will allow adversity in your life in order to reveal Himself to you and to show where you have created idols out of the things that provide you with guidance, security, and prosperity. He wants you to let go of them so He can have first place in your life and raise you up to the highest, best, and strongest your life can be.

Third, fight your battles on your knees—in humility before the Lord your God.

As you go to your Father in prayer, recall Ecclesiastes 5:1–2:

Guard your steps as you go to the house of God and draw near to listen rather than to offer the sacrifice of fools; for they do not know they are doing evil. Do not be hasty in word or impulsive in thought to bring up a matter in the presence of God. For God is in heaven and you are on the earth; therefore let your words be few.

Remember who it is you are approaching and don't try to solve the problems on your own. God will show you what to do. But go before Him with a reverent and submitted heart, because He will certainly direct you in ways that you've probably never considered. Be an active listener so He can prepare you for and lead you on the right path.

Fourth, diligently sow trust and obedience in your life.

In prayer, in Bible study, in your interactions with others, and in decisions—always remember that your goal is to know God, honor Him, and walk in His ways. Why? Because as we learned in Hebrews 11:6, every choice we make comes back to: *Do we believe that God exists? Do we have confidence that He is a rewarder of those who seek Him?*

These are the questions before you through each and every trial and challenge you face: Do you really trust the Lord's character? Do you have confidence that He is working all things for your good? Because every decision you make is like a seed planted in your life, either nurturing your relationship with the Father or destroying it. And as you know, you reap what you sow, more than you sow, and later than you sow. Galatians 6:8 promises, "The one who sows to the Spirit"—or obedience to God—"will from the Spirit reap eternal life."

Therefore, always look beyond your immediate choices to the

consequences that will follow and understand that each decision is a step in a long progression—growing your faith in ways and for purposes you could never imagine.

Fifth, accept that the challenge you're facing is hitting you where you are weak, so that the Holy Spirit can pour out His life through you and be strong on your behalf.

The Lord God has resurrection power for you. We see this in Ephesians 1:19–20, where we are assured that "the surpassing greatness of His power" is available to "us who believe." This is the same "working of the strength of His might which He brought about in Christ, when He raised Him from the dead."

However, His resurrection power can flow through you only when you stop fighting Him—trying to do things on your own—and accept that it is not about your glory, but His.

In 2 Corinthians 4:7, we are reminded that "we have this treasure in earthen vessels, so that the surpassing greatness of the power will be of God and not from ourselves." In other words, the Lord makes sure that people can see He is the One at work, because His ultimate goal is to draw others to Himself.

Friend, God wants you and others to see that He is indeed *real*. Why? Because then you will realize who God really is and that He is worthy to call you, lead you, and provide for you. Because then you can release control of your life to Him, understanding that when you do, you will experience a *better* life—an indestructible, victorious resurrected life. And what He will accomplish through you will truly last forever (1 John 2:17).

Sixth, make sure that you not only remain in fellowship with other believers, but that you are actively seeking to pour Christ's life into them.

Remember that a strong life is lived in relationship with other believers. Because it is in your interactions with the Body of Christ that you are reminded

+ *of your worth.* You are valuable because of the price Jesus paid for you.

+ *that you belong.* You are an important and a permanent member of God's family.

+ *that you are competent.* You are capable of carrying out the unique tasks the Father planned in advance for you to do (Eph. 2:10).

A strong life isn't just about what happens to you; it's also about whom you have around you and how you're edifying them—how you are supporting and protecting each other, joining with others in worship, learning the Word of God, exercising spiritual gifts with one another, and fulfilling the Great Commission together. So you not only make your life stronger by serving, but you also make the Body of Christ healthier, more vital, and more robust by your faithful participation. You never know who will inspire you or whom you will encourage as you walk through the storms of life with other believers.

Finally, see everything that happens as coming from God Himself for the very purpose of making you stronger.

This is one of the most important principles you can learn: *The Father has allowed the challenges in your life for your benefit.* Every trial you experience is supposed to be a bridge to a deeper relationship with the Lord and will ultimately "perfect, confirm, strengthen and establish you" if you trust the Father in it (1 Pet. 5:10).

Why? Because it reminds you that "God causes all things to work together for good to those who love God, to those who are called according to His purpose" (Rom. 8:28).

Instead of seeing the storms that rise against you as a burden, you understand that your loving heavenly Father has planned some special blessing for you through them—that the difficulties you face will ultimately bring you good and will give Him glory, if you'll continue to walk in faith and obedience with Him.

So whenever you face a battle, ask God,

+ What is Your goal for allowing this to happen in my life? What do You want me to learn?

+ Are You leading me into a deeper relationship with Yourself?

+ Are You setting me free from the bondage to sin?

+ Are You conforming me to the likeness of Christ's character?

+ Are You strengthening my faith?

+ Are You leading me into a greater understanding of obedience?

+ Are You preparing me to minister to others?

+ Are You increasing my effectiveness for Your Kingdom?

‣ Are You cleaning out what is inhibiting the resurrection-life of Christ from flowing through me?

Listen carefully to Him. Because certainly He will answer you, and you will end up praising Him for the very troubles that once caused you such grief.

THE IMAGE OF JESUS IN YOU

Friend, always remember that in order for God to strengthen you to the point of doing great things through you, He must ready you for His service by forming the very image of Jesus in you: His freedom, character, confidence, obedience, heart, focus, mission, and power.

This is a difficult and often painful process, but do not despair. God is not allowing adversity in your life in order to devastate or discourage you—though that may be how it feels. Rather, He does so for the express purpose of making sure that you build your life with "gold, silver, precious stones"—those materials worthy of one who belongs to Jesus (1 Cor. 3:12–13).

So take heart and understand for certain that your Savior is not trying to defeat you through the adversity before you today. On the contrary, He is making certain that you will "overwhelmingly conquer through Him who loved" you (Rom. 8:37).

10

YOUR CONVICTIONS ABOUT THE END

Looking Toward His Kingdom

The truth of the matter is that within every human heart is the longing to stand strong and have an impact that endures far beyond our own lifetimes. For our stories to end well. For our lives to have a lasting influence on this world and beyond. We want to know that the days we've lived and the difficulties we've suffered were not in vain—that they actually made a difference. We want to be certain that what we are standing for is worthwhile.

This is not something that is unique to believers, of course. You can see it everywhere you go—legislation, highways, college buildings, and medical wings all bear the names of people who saw a future beyond themselves. And if you ever felt the joy of seeing your own name etched into something lasting or the pain of seeing what you worked to achieve dismantled, perhaps you've understood this in your own heart as well.

Ecclesiastes 3:11 explains this by saying that God has set eternity in the heart of every person. I believe that this is a desire not just to live forever but also to be known forever—to have a positive impact that is recognized by others.

Thankfully, as believers we know that everything we do in obedience to God does, indeed, carry on. Philippians 1:6 promises, "I am confident of this very thing, that He who began a good work in you will perfect it until the day of Christ Jesus." In other words, what Jesus does in and through you has lasting fruit that continues to increase and grow until He returns (John 15:16). Furthermore, Ecclesiastes 3:14 assures us, "I know that everything God does will remain forever." As we've discussed repeatedly throughout the pages of this book, nothing we do in submission to Him will ever truly fade away (1 John 2:17).

> *Having eternity in our hearts is a desire not just to live forever but also to be known forever—to have a positive impact that is recognized by others.*

A LESSON FROM GRANDDAD

I was particularly struck by the enduring quality our lives can have as I traveled back to my hometown of Dry Fork, Virginia, to celebrate the one hundredth anniversary of Emmanuel Pentecostal Holiness Church—a church my grandfather George Washington Stanley planted. In 1915, Granddad was invited to hold a revival there by ten believers who had been meeting as a house church. He set up his tent at the corner of Johnson Road and Dry Fork Road and preached his heart out. Ultimately, the church grew to thirty-five members. The next year, in November 1916, that small group of believers invited my grandfather back to be pastor and he accepted.

Granddad was only pastor of Emmanuel Pentecostal Holiness Church until 1921, but you should hear how they still talk about his impact on the congregation and community. As I walked through the church, one person after another grabbed my arm to tell me how Granddad had influenced his or her family—how he'd led a dying loved one to the Lord, how God had done miracles of healing through him, and how he'd changed Dry Fork for the better. It touched me deeply how the families there had passed down the stories from one generation to another. But what struck me even more profoundly was the spiritual legacy that continued in that congregation. After one hundred years, it was still healthy, still thriving, still faithful to God's Word, and still reaching people with the gospel.

I have often told of how spending a week with him when I was sixteen changed the course of my life—teaching me that the most important thing I could ever do is prioritize my relationship with God. During six transformative days in 1949, Granddad taught me the four principles that formed the foundation of my spiritual life:

- Obey God and leave all the consequences to Him.

- God will move heaven and earth to reveal His will to you if you truly want to know it and carry it out.

- God will provide for all your needs.

- God will protect you.

AN ANSWER FOR THE LONGING

I say all this because the Lord has an answer to that longing we all have in our hearts that our lives will leave an eternal legacy. All He requires is that we be faithful to Him. Understand, Granddad wasn't educated, wealthy, or of a prominent social standing. On the contrary, Granddad taught himself to read by reading the Bible. In his early days, he made his living cutting railroad ties, which was difficult work for very little money. And he preached against the use of tobacco in a region where it was the main cash crop—so he wasn't politically powerful by any means.

In fact, if there was anything that characterized my grandfather's life, it was difficulty. Yet, in his unpublished autobiography, "My Life's Experiences for God," Granddad wrote:

> I am not sorry that my trials here have been hard, because I know it means a brighter crown in the land where I shall lay my burdens down at the feet of my Lord. I have often wondered what difference it makes about one's life here, just so long as it is spent so that when the breath is taken from the body he knows that God will say: "Well done thou good and faithful servant. Thou has been faithful over a few things, I shall make thee ruler over many."

Granddad didn't have anything you don't have; in fact, he surely had less. Rather, what set Granddad apart—and every disciple who ever serves God (Acts 4:13)—is Jesus. It was the Lord who worked through him to plant eighteen churches in Virginia and North Carolina and affect countless lives for eternity. Granddad died in 1964, but because of what Jesus did in and through him, his influence remains forever. And I am certain that the Lord is rewarding all the loving faithfulness Granddad demonstrated in ways beyond imagination.

God can work through you, too. You can have a legacy that lasts, though this world and even time itself might pass away. And it all begins in your own home. Psalm 78:1–8 instructs:

> Listen, O my people, to my instruction; incline your ears to the words of my mouth. I will open my mouth in a parable; I will utter dark sayings of old, which we have heard and known, and our fathers have told us. We will not conceal them from their children, but tell to the generation to come the praises of the Lord, and His strength and His wondrous works that He has done. For He established a testimony in Jacob and appointed a law in Israel, which He commanded our fathers that they should teach them to their children, that the generation to come might know, even the children yet to be born, that they may arise and tell them to their children, that they should put their confidence in God and not forget the works of God, but keep His commandments.

As believers, we have a divine obligation to teach our children and those who come after us the truth of God's Word so that they'll know the Savior, realize He has a plan for their lives, and understand that He will equip them for everything He calls them to accomplish. In other words, so they can have strong, godly lives. Of course, God tells us to reach our families first because this is the main platform He has provided for influence. Members of a family have a bond that makes communicating these spiritual principles natural and effective. For example, my granddaughter Annie recently asked me to repeat the stories about my grandfather so she could teach them to her young sons. Why? Because she's seen these principles work in my life and knows it would benefit her sons to live by them as well.

CHANGING THE LANDSCAPE OF ETERNITY

Now, I realize that we discussed this in part when we talked about our role in the Body of Christ. But I cannot stress enough that you truly stand strong only when you are faithfully passing on your faith.

Think about it: This is the basis by which the stories of the Old Testament were passed down from generation to generation. When Psalm 78 was written, there were no printing presses or any of the resources we have now to transmit information and educate our children. Though there were records kept by scribes, for the most part the stories were passed on orally—one faithful life to another. The people of Israel obeyed God's command, "These words, which I am commanding you today, shall be on your heart. You shall teach them diligently to your sons and shall talk of them when you sit in your house and when you walk by the way and when you lie down and when you rise up" (Deut. 6:6–7).

When I consider how these accounts of God's faithfulness endured through the centuries despite wars, famines, exiles, and the rest, I am both in awe and inspired. We may not know all the names of those who were committed to passing on His Word, but we continue to benefit from their strong lives.

With this in view, we see there is something very powerful about telling a loved one about what God has done, handing down our personal testimony of His loving-kindness and wisdom both in word and deed. But the best news is: Our godly example and testimony are enough to change the landscape of eternity—not only for those in our families but also for the countless others they, too, will influence.

However, as you read this you may be thinking, *I don't have that kind of relationship with my family. Does that mean I cannot have a spiritual legacy?* Or perhaps you don't have children and wonder what that means for you. The family is the starting point in our quest to impact eternity, but it certainly isn't the end point. This is why it's important for you to have a sense of the long, unbroken line of faithfulness that led to your knowing Jesus as your Savior. From the time Jesus spoke to the first disciples until you heard and accepted the Good News of salvation, it was one person who faithfully told the next until it reached you. Sometimes it was through family members, yes. But at other times it was through friendships, through chance meetings, through business relationships, through sermons, through books, and countless other ways that one person expressed to another the great gift of salvation that is available through Jesus Christ.

There is a great deal of beauty and awe in that. There is also a great responsibility to touch the hearts of the next generation and pass on the mandate. As Romans 10:14 asks, "How will they believe in Him whom they have not heard? And how will they hear without a preacher?"

Taking Up the Holy Task of
Building His Kingdom

Thankfully, for those who willingly, courageously, and wisely take up the holy task to build a strong foundation and construct their lives with the materials that honor God, the enduring legacy grows and becomes increasingly more impactful as those who come behind them follow in their footsteps (Prov. 11:30).

What do I mean by that? It's what we saw in Jesus' words, "Truly, truly, I say to you, he who believes in Me, the works that I do, he will do also; and greater works than these he will do; because I go to the Father" (John 14:12). The works become greater and greater as they go from one person to the next.

And that is how we must see our own lives. My grandfather influenced me, so he has also had an effect on everyone I've ever spoken to about Jesus. And as each person I influence speaks to others, my grandfather's impact becomes exponentially more vast and powerful. In this way, we see that if we are truly serving Jesus, those who follow after us grow our spiritual legacy in a manner beyond imagination, with joy unspeakable.

My grandfather wrote of his own heavenly vision: "In the end, may you, too, see God, so that on yonder streets of gold we shall rejoice together and again be reunited with loved ones and friends. There we shall live forever with our God." What better goal could anyone have?

Friend, like George Washington Stanley, you simply cannot go wrong when you invest in a future beyond yourself by devoting yourself to Christ and telling your family, your friends, your coworkers, and everyone you meet about what God has done. That's what Granddad did, and I still see the fruit of his faithfulness.

There is no telling how profoundly you can impact eternity each time you share Jesus with others. However, one thing is sure: You are indeed leaving a legacy that stands strong and persists far beyond you, one you can be proud of and that will certainly influence what you do in the Kingdom to come.

And when you do enter that Kingdom, you too will hear, "Well done, good and faithful servant," like my grandfather.

LIVE FOR HIM; REIGN WITH HIM

Of course, we may wonder at what the Lord Jesus says here: "You were faithful over a few things, I will make you ruler over many things. Enter into the joy of your lord" (Matt. 25:21 NKJV). This speaks to something further that awaits us when we see our Savior face-to-face. In fact, we are also promised rewards for obedience and commitment in His coming Kingdom. We are told in 2 Corinthians 5:10, "We must all appear before the judgment seat of Christ, so that each one may be recompensed for his deeds in the body, according to what he has done, whether good or bad."

What are the rewards? Certainly not all will have the same privileges and responsibilities. But we do know from Scripture that some will receive crowns:

+ *The Incorruptible Crown* (1 Cor. 9:25–27) is given to believers who, like athletes, are disciplined in order to be the best for Jesus they can be. Regardless of the obstacles, they continue to steadfastly trust and obey God in all things and refuse to disqualify themselves by giving in to sin.

+ *The Crown of Rejoicing* (1 Thess. 2:19–20) is given to believers who have taken part in leading others to Christ by proclaiming the gospel.

+ *The Crown of Righteousness* (2 Tim. 4:7–8) is given to believers who live godly lives because they are anticipating Jesus' return. Their focus is on Christ and His Kingdom rather than on earthly rewards.

+ *The Crown of Life* (James 1:2; Rev. 2:10) is given to believers who remain faithful to Jesus despite being persecuted for their faith.

+ *The Crown of Glory* (1 Pet. 5:1–4) is given to believers who have been leaders in the church and have faithfully shepherded the people of God—being good examples and spurring others on to love and good deeds.

Likewise, from the seven letters to the seven churches in Revelation 2–3, we know there are rewards for those who persevere and are "children of God above reproach in the midst of a crooked and perverse generation, among whom you appear as lights in the world" (Phil. 2:15). In other words, good things are in store for those who remain faithful despite the challenges:

+ "To him who overcomes, I will grant to eat of the tree of life which is in the Paradise of God" (Rev. 2:7).

- ✦ "He who overcomes will not be hurt by the second death" (Rev. 2:11).

- ✦ "To him who overcomes, to him I will give some of the hidden manna, and I will give him a white stone, and a new name written on the stone which no one knows but he who receives it" (Rev. 2:17).

- ✦ "He who overcomes, and he who keeps My deeds until the end, to him I will give authority over the nations; and he shall rule them with a rod of iron" (Rev. 2:26–27).

- ✦ "He who overcomes will thus be clothed in white garments; and I will not erase his name from the book of life, and I will confess his name before My Father and before His angels" (Rev. 3:5).

- ✦ "He who overcomes, I will make him a pillar in the temple of My God, and he will not go out from it anymore; and I will write on him the name of My God, and the name of the city of My God, the new Jerusalem, which comes down out of heaven from My God, and My new name" (Rev. 3:12).

- ✦ "He who overcomes, I will grant to him to sit down with Me on My throne, as I also overcame and sat down with My Father on His throne" (Rev. 3:21).

We may not understand all of those blessings, but they are certainly worthwhile. And that last reward is particularly intriguing. In fact, Revelation 20:6 tells us, "Blessed and holy is the one who has a part in the first resurrection; over these the second death has no power, *but they will be priests of God and of Christ and will reign with Him for a thousand years"* (emphasis added). In other words, those who know Jesus and serve Him faithfully here will reign with Him in His Millennial Kingdom.

Likewise, we learn in 2 Timothy 2:11–12, "If we died with Him"—that is, live for Jesus here on earth—"we will also live with Him; if we endure, we will also reign with Him."

Now, these are striking promises. Think about it: The most respected and powerful people in Christ's coming Kingdom will be the ones who have proved themselves most obedient, wise, and faithful here on earth. That gives us an amazing motivation to live a strong life in the center of God's will while we have breath in our lungs. We may live here sixty, eighty, one hundred years, but it is merely the blinking of an eye compared to what awaits us in eternity.

But please take note: We will not rule with Him there unless we submit ourselves to Him here (Matt. 16:24–26). And we cannot truly yield ourselves to Him unless we lay our foundation on Christ and build with that which honors Him (1 Cor. 3:11–15).

So the challenge for us today is to realize that even at this very moment we are setting the tone for eternity. We must be willing to give Jesus our very best because we want to please Him, exalt Him, and have everything we do be judged as worthy by Him. And if we do, He will certainly honor us (Heb. 6:9–11).

ENDING STRONG

So friend, regardless of why you picked up this book on standing strong—whether a storm is raging in your life, you are preparing for one on the horizon, or you simply wish to be a success—make sure you are constructing your life with the only foundation that never crumbles and the materials that will not burn up on the day of judgment. Make sure your story ends well.

Build it *on* . . .

+ *the Word of God*—the unbreakable rock of truth, which has withstood the hurricane winds and torrential rains of time.

+ *the God you can know*—the omnipotent, omniscient, omnipresent, and omnibenevolent Lord of creation, who loves you, desires to reveal Himself to you, and teaches you to walk in His ways.

+ *His salvation and the intimacy He offers you*—the relationship that gives your life significance, characterizes your life with peace, fills you with unshakable joy, and gives your life an enduring impact.

+ *prayer*—your unending conversation with the living God wherein He reveals Himself and His plans for your life.

And build it *with* . . .

+ *trust and obedience*—the two pillars of an increasingly strong, fruitful, and faithful life.

+ *Christ's resurrection-life*—His supernatural, abundant, indestructible presence in the world through the Holy Spirit, who is able to accomplish above and beyond all we can ask or imagine (Eph. 3:20).

+ *others*—continuing that unbroken line of relationships that began with Christ and will endure throughout eternity.

+ *the understanding that with adversity you're facing a bridge to a deeper relationship with Him*—building Christ's own freedom, character, confidence, obedience, heart, focus, mission, and power in you.

Because when you do, you'll certainly have the strong life you long for. And like my grandfather, you will be able to say that "it has been a life full of heartache and pain; yet, through Jesus Christ, it has been enriched with happiness, joy, and love. Sometimes I have wondered why things have happened the way they have. Yet, in the end, it all worked out for good."

Amen to that.

NOTES

1. www.chabad.org/library/article_cdo/aid/352329/jewish/The-Walls-of-the-Study-Hall.htm.
2. Charles H. Spurgeon, *The Autobiography*, Susannah Spurgeon and Joseph Harrald, eds. (New York: F. H. Revell, 1896), vol. 1, p. 105.
3. Ibid., pp. 105–6.
4. George Müller, *Answers to Prayer: From George Müller's Narratives* (Chicago: Moody Publishers, 1896), pp. 17–18.
5. Watchman Nee, *Sit, Walk, Stand: The Process of Christian Maturity* (Wheaton, IL: Tyndale House, 1977), pp. 72–73.
6. Ibid., pp. 73–74.
7. Ibid., p. 74.
8. Ibid., p. 76.
9. R. A. Torrey, *The Holy Spirit: Who He Is and What He Does* (Alachua, FL: Bridge-Logos, 2008), p. 32.

PERSONAL NOTES

_____

_____

_____

_____

_____

_____

_____

_____

_____

_____

PERSONAL NOTES

_____

_____

_____

_____

_____

_____

_____

_____

_____

_____

_____

_____

_____

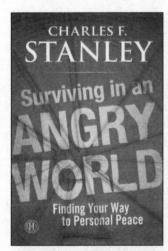
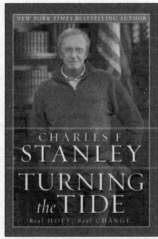
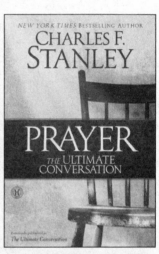

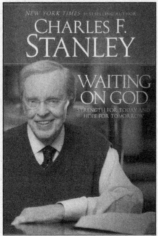
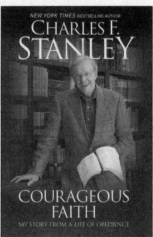

Start your day with the Lord.

Life can be hectic. There are schedules to juggle, deadlines to meet, and family activities to manage. But each morning comes with a new opportunity to draw closer to the Lord.

Start your day off right with an encouraging and uplifting devotion delivered straight to your inbox, ready for you as you prepare to take on the day. Subscribe for free at **intouch.org/subscriptions**.